Letters
from
God

Presented To:

_____

Presented By:

_____

Date:

_____

Letters
from
God

God's Faithful Promises for You

HARVEST HOUSE™ PUBLISHERS
EUGENE, OREGON

Letters from God

ISBN 0-7369-1253-3
Copyright © 2000 by GRQ Ink, Inc.

Published by **Harvest House Publishers**
Eugene, OR 97402
www.harvesthousepublishers.com

Developed by GRQ Ink, Inc.
Manuscript written by Melody Carlson
Cover design, interior design, and composition by
Whisner Design Group, Tulsa, Oklahoma

Printed in China. 03 04 05 06 07 08 09 / RDS / 7 6 5 4 3 2 1

A Letter from God

Dear One,

Oh, how I long to speak to you. How I desire to reveal My endless and perfect love for you. How I long for you to experience My goodness and understanding, My great care and compassion.

Do you know how much My heart hungers to speak directly to your heart? Have you any idea how I wait for you to come to Me? How I long for you to know that I am ready to speak and eager to listen. For I have infinite words of wisdom and direction for your life. And I long to guide and encourage you on a daily basis.

So, come to Me and listen to My words. Learn from Me and fully experience My never-ending love for you.

All My love,

Your Heavenly Father

I will instruct you and train you in the way you shall go; I will counsel you with My eye on you.
Psalm 32:8 MLB

Contents

My Love for You

*My love for you is perfect,
unconditional—and forever.*

Dear Beloved,

I know how you have longed for love. I have watched you seek it from those who should have loved you and from those who didn't even care. And all the while I was waiting—always ready to wrap My arms of love around you and gather you to Myself. My love for you began so long ago—way back when I formed you in your mother's womb. And long ago, I loved you as a child; and sometimes you even knew it. I've loved you through all your heartbreaks and disappointments and triumphs. And I loved you even when you didn't love yourself—or Me.

My love for you, unlike a human love, is perfect; and I will continue to love you no matter what. And, yes, My child, I will love you always and forever.

With never-ending love,

Your Heavenly Father

We have known and believed the love that
God has for us. God is love, and he who
abides in love abides in God, and God
in him.
1 John 4:16 NKJV

I love them that love me; and those that
seek me early shall find me.
Proverbs 8:17 KJV

God proves his love for us in that while we still
were sinners Christ died for us.
Romans 5:8 NRSV

Day by day the Lord also pours out his steadfast
love upon me, and through the night I sing his
songs and pray to God who gives me life.
Psalm 42:8 TLB

I am persuaded that neither death nor life, nor
angels nor principalities nor powers, nor things
present nor things to come, nor height nor depth,
nor any other created thing, shall be able to
separate us from the love of God which is in Christ
Jesus our Lord.
Romans 8:38-39 NKJV

God, who is rich in mercy, because of His great love
with which He loved us, even when we were dead
in trespasses, made us alive together with Christ (by
grace you have been saved).
Ephesians 2:4 NKJV

Love

Long ago the Lord had said to Israel: I
have loved you, O my people, with an
everlasting love; with loving-kindness I
have drawn you to me.
Jeremiah 31:3 TLB

Keep yourselves in the love of God; look
forward to the mercy of our Lord Jesus
Christ that leads to eternal life.
Jude 21 NRSV

I trust in your unfailing love;
my heart rejoices in your salvation.
Psalm 13:5 NIV

"The mountains shall depart
and the hills be removed,
but My kindness shall not depart
from you, nor shall My covenant
of peace be removed,"
says the LORD, who has mercy on you.
Isaiah 54:10 NKJV

God's love has been poured into our hearts through the Holy Spirit that has been given to us.
Romans 5:5 NRSV

O LORD, God of Israel, there is no God like you in heaven or on earth—you who keep your covenant of love with your servants who continue wholeheartedly in your way.
2 Chronicles 6:14 NIV

I will be glad and rejoice in your love, for you saw my affliction and knew the anguish of my soul.
Psalm 31:7 NIV

Let them give thanks to the LORD for His lovingkindness, and for His wonders to the sons of men! For He has satisfied the thirsty soul, and the hungry soul He has filled with what is good.
Psalm 107:8-9 NAS

I will betroth thee unto me for ever; yea, I will betroth thee unto me in righteousness, and in judgment, and in lovingkindness, and in mercies. I will even betroth thee unto me in faithfulness: and thou shalt know the LORD.
Hosea 2:19-20 KJV

My Gift of Peace

*My peace is more precious
than all the world's riches.*

Dear Child of Mine,

I understand your desire for peace. But sometimes, dear one, you confuse peace with escape. You think that life would be much more peaceful if only you could simply get away from all your problems.

But My peace isn't like that. My peace is like snuggling into a sturdily built house during a raging hurricane. The storm outside may bluster and blow, but the immovable house will keep you safe from all harm.

To experience My peace, you must first trust Me with your heart and your life. And even when you feel anxious, you must keep your faith anchored securely in Me, your loving Father. Do these simple things, and you will no longer need to search for peace. It will begin to flow from deep inside you.

Shalom,

The Prince of Peace

Peace I leave with you, My peace I give to you; not as the world gives do I give to you.
John 14:27 NKJV

Keep on doing the things that you have learned and received and heard and seen in me, and the God of peace will be with you.
Philippians 4:9 NRSV

The LORD will give strength to His people;
The LORD will bless His people with peace.
Psalm 29:11 NKJV

You will keep him in perfect peace,
Whose mind is stayed on You,
Because he trusts in You.
Isaiah 26:3 NKJV

Since we are justified by faith, we have
peace with God through our Lord Jesus
Christ.
Romans 5:1 NRSV

May the God of peace himself make you
entirely pure and devoted to God; and
may your spirit and soul and body be kept
strong and blameless until that day when
our Lord Jesus Christ comes back again.
1 Thessalonians 5:23 TLB

Peace

The God of peace be with all of you.
Amen.
Romans 15:33 NRSV

Turn from all known sin and spend your
time in doing good. Try to live in peace
with everyone; work hard at it.
Psalm 34:14 TLB

Aim for perfection, listen to my appeal, be
of one mind, live in peace. And the God of
love and peace will be with you.
2 Corinthians 13:11 NIV

Live in peace with each other. Do not be
proud, but make friends with those who
seem unimportant. Do not think how
smart you are.
Romans 12:16 NCV

All who listen to me will live in peace and
safety, unafraid of harm.
Proverbs 1:33 NLT

Finally, brethren, rejoice, be made
complete, be comforted, be like-minded,
live in peace; and the God of love and
peace will be with you.
2 Corinthians 13:11 NAS

When people live so that they please the
LORD, even their enemies will make peace
with them.
Proverbs 16:7 NCV

Hold them in the highest regard in love
because of their work. Live in peace with
each other.
1 Thessalonians 5:13 NIV

I will hear what God the LORD will speak,
For He will speak peace
To His people and to His saints;
But let them not turn back to folly.
Psalm 85:8 NKJV

A harvest of righteousness is sown in
peace for those who make peace.
James 3:18 NRSV

The peace of God, which passeth all
understanding, shall keep your hearts and
minds through Christ Jesus.
Philippians 4:7 KJV

I Will Walk with You

I promise you My constant companionship.

Dear Blessed One,

I know your deep desire for one true friend—someone who will never disappoint you, never let you down. A companion who will always be available to listen, able to understand, and ready to comfort. But no such earthly person exists. No, not even you can provide that level of perfect friendship to another. It's just not humanly possible.

But what is impossible with man is possible with Me. For I am God. And, oh how I long to be that kind of friend to you. I want to share in every aspect of your life—both the good and the bad. I long to listen and to help you through life's challenges.

So, come to Me, and allow Me to be your one true friend—that constant companion who will never leave or disappoint you. I will be waiting.

Your Best Friend,

The Lord God

I will ask the Father, and he will give you
another Counselor, who will never
leave you.
John 14:16 NLT

No man shall be able to stand before you all the days of your life; as I was with Moses, so I will be with you. I will not leave you nor forsake you.
Joshua 1:5 NKJV

If we are faithless,
he will remain faithful,
for he cannot disown himself.
2 Timothy 2:13 NIV

The LORD himself goes before you and will
be with you; he will never leave you nor
forsake you. Do not be afraid;
do not be discouraged.
Deuteronomy 31:8 NIV

To the praise of the glory of His grace, which
He freely bestowed on us in the Beloved.
Ephesians 1:6 NAS

He did not leave Himself without witness, in
that He did good and gave you rains from
heaven and fruitful seasons, satisfying your
hearts with food and gladness.
Acts 14:17 NAS

Companionship

So rejoice, O sons of Zion,
And be glad in the LORD your God;
For He has given you the early rain
for your vindication.
And He has poured down for you the rain,
The early and latter rain as before.
Joel 2:23 NAS

My God shall supply all your need according
to His riches in glory by Christ Jesus.
Philippians 4:19 NKJV

The LORD is my shepherd; I shall not want.
Psalm 23:1 KJV

He provides food for those who fear him; he
remembers his covenant forever.
Psalm 111:5 NIV

I will satiate the soul of the priests
with abundance,
and My people shall be satisfied with My
goodness, says the LORD.
Jeremiah 31:14 NKJV

Praise be to the Lord, to God our Savior,
who daily bears our burdens.
Psalm 68:19 NIV

We may boldly say, The LORD is my helper, and I will not fear what man shall do unto me.
Hebrews 13:6 KJV

Let us hold unswervingly to the hope we profess, for he who promised is faithful.
Hebrews 10:23 NIV

Be strong and courageous, do not be afraid or tremble at them, for the LORD your God is the one who goes with you. He will not fail you or forsake you.
Deuteronomy 31:6 NAS

The LORD will guide you continually,
And satisfy your soul in drought,
And strengthen your bones;
You shall be like a watered garden,
And like a spring of water, whose waters do not fail.
Isaiah 58:11 NKJV

Which of you, if his son asks for bread, will give him a stone? Or if he asks for a fish, will give him a snake? If you, then, though you are evil, know how to give good gifts to your children, how much more will your Father in heaven give good gifts to those who ask him!
Matthew 7:9-11 NIV

My Power and Strength

*You cannot fathom the
strength I long to give
to you.*

My Own,

I know how you've always longed to be a strong person. I fully realize how you desire more power in your life. And it's not that you are powerless, for you make choices for yourself every day. But it is never enough, is it? You always long for more.

If you really do want more strength and power, I urge you to identify your areas of weakness—those places where you struggle. As you ask for My help and allow Me to become involved in those areas, you will find that your weaknesses will soon become your strengths. How is that possible? Even in those areas where you feel strong and powerful, you alone cannot match what the two of us can do together. Call on Me. I am longing to help you.

In power and strength,

The Almighty

He said to me, "My grace is sufficient
for you, for My strength is made perfect
in weakness."
2 Corinthians 12:9 NKJV

That He may grant you, in keeping with the wealth of His glory, to be empowered with strength in the inner self by His Spirit.
Ephesians 3:16 MLB

My soul melteth for heaviness: strengthen thou me according unto thy word.
Psalm 119:28 KJV

That your faith might not rest in the wisdom of men but in the power of God.
1 Corinthians 2:5 RSV

And into an inheritance that can never perish, spoil or fade—kept in heaven for you, who through faith are shielded by God's power until the coming of the salvation that is ready to be revealed in the last time.
1 Peter 1:4-5 NIV

Because of his strength I will watch for You, for God is my stronghold. My God in His lovingkindness will meet me; God will let me look triumphantly upon my foes.
Psalm 59:9-10 NAS

21

Power

The LORD is my strength and my song;
he has become my salvation.
He is my God, and I will praise him,
my father's God, and I will exalt him.
Exodus 15:2 NIV

I am not ashamed of the gospel, for it is
the power of God for salvation to
everyone who believes, to the Jew
first and also to the Greek.
Romans 1:16 NAS

You are my hiding place; you will protect
me from trouble and surround me
with songs of deliverance.
Psalm 32:7 NIV

The eternal God is a dwelling place, and
underneath are the everlasting arms;
And He drove out the enemy from
before you, and said, "Destroy!"
Deuteronomy 33:27 NAS

The Lord is faithful, and He will strengthen
and protect you from the evil one.
2 Thessalonians 3:3 NAS

I will teach you about the power of
God and will not hide the ways of the
Almighty.
Job 27:11 NCV

O LORD, be gracious to us;
we long for you.
Be our strength every morning,
our salvation in time of distress.
Isaiah 33:2 NIV

The LORD preserves all who love Him,
But all the wicked He will destroy.
Psalm 145:20 NKJV

My flesh and my heart may fail,
but God is the strength of my heart and
my portion forever.
Psalm 73:26 NAS

God is our refuge and strength, a very
present help in trouble.
Psalm 46:1 KJV

Do not fear, for I am with you; do not be
dismayed, for I am your God. I will
strengthen you and help you; I will uphold
you with my righteous right hand.
Isaiah 41:10 NIV

My Ways Are Higher

*My will isn't always your
will, but it's best.*

Dear One Whom I Love,

You sometimes think you know what's best—
and in many situations you are absolutely right.
But not always. For your knowledge and
experience are limited by your humanity. You
cannot see beyond the here and now as I can. Nor
can you fathom all the great and wonderful plans
I have for you.

So instead of questioning why I do the things
I do (and I know it can seem confusing), I hope
you'll come to accept that I want only what's best
for you. My plan for your life is far more
wonderful, more fulfilling than anything you can
imagine. So, come to Me. Place your trust in Me,
and I will reveal great things to you—one
wonderful step at a time.

In all wisdom,

The Alpha and Omega

The Lord is King and rules the nations.
Psalm 22:28 TLB

When I consider Your heavens, the work of Your fingers, the moon and the stars, which You have ordained, what is man that You are mindful of him, and the son of man that You visit him? For You have made him a little lower than the angels, and You have crowned him with glory and honor.
Psalm 8:3-5 NKJV

The LORD will always lead you. He will satisfy your needs in dry lands and give strength to your bones. You will be like a garden that has much water, like a spring that never runs dry.
Isaiah 58:11 NCV

Every day and all night long their counsel will lead you and save you from harm; when you wake up in the morning, let their instructions guide you into the new day.
Proverbs 6:22 TLB

I Will Be with You

*I can carve a path through
the toughest terrain.*

My Own,

I know there are times when you feel lost and alone. Whether that feeling is the result of bad choices on your part or just uncontrollable circumstances, I want you to know that I am always with you, watching over you, loving you. Just call out to Me, and I will be there.

The circumstances in which you find yourself may not change. But I can promise that you will never be alone, for I will never leave you. And you will never be lost, for I will be walking by your side, guiding your steps, showing you the way. Keep your eyes on Me and your ears tuned to My voice. We will walk together until we reach a place of safety.

On My way,

Your Deliverer

Everyone born of God overcomes the
world. This is the victory that has
overcome the world, even our faith.
1 John 5:4 NIV

Surely He shall deliver you from the snare of the fowler and from the perilous pestilence.
Psalm 91:3 NKJV

Out of his glorious, unlimited resources he will give you the mighty inner strengthening of his Holy Spirit.
Ephesians 3:16 TLB

Call upon me in the day of trouble;
I will deliver you, and you will honor me.
Psalm 50:15 NIV

I can do all things through Christ who strengthens me.
Philippians 4:13 NKJV

I will sing of thy power; yea, I will sing aloud of thy mercy in the morning: for thou hast been my defence and refuge in the day of my trouble.
Psalm 59:16 KJV

You are my hiding place;
You preserve me from trouble;
You surround me with songs of deliverance.
Psalm 32:7 NAS

Trust in Me

Bring your heart to Me.

Dear Child,

I know you struggle with issues of trust. And it's never easy to put your life into the hands of another. What if they fail you or use you or hurt you? And what about those who've already disappointed you—couldn't it happen again?

But it's not that way with Me, dear one. For I will never let you down. I cannot—for I am God. I will never abandon you. I will never forsake you. My love for you is as constant as the rising and setting of the sun—and even more so. And so, I ask you to trust Me—not just a little and not just for a while. But reach out to Me with your whole heart and rest in My love for the rest of your days. I am waiting to show you who I am—and how completely worthy I am of your trust.

Trust Me,

The Lord of All

He will not let your foot slip—he who
watches over you will not slumber.
Psalm 121:3 NIV

Trust in the LORD with all your heart,
and lean not on your own understanding;
in all your ways acknowledge Him, and
He shall direct your paths.
Proverbs 3:5-6 NKJV

May the God of hope fill you with all joy
and peace as you trust in him, so that you
may overflow with hope by the power of
the Holy Spirit.
Romans 15:13 NIV

By awesome deeds You answer us in
righteousness, O God of our salvation,
You who are the trust of all the ends of
the earth and of the farthest sea.
Psalm 65:5 NAS

Fear of man is a dangerous trap, but to
trust in God means safety.
Proverbs 29:25 TLB

Trust

Put your trust in the Lord, and offer him
pleasing sacrifices.
Psalm 4:5 TLB

Those who know the LORD trust him,
because he will not leave those who come to
him.
Psalm 9:10 NCV

Through Christ you have come to trust in
God. And because God raised Christ
from the dead and gave him great glory, your
faith and hope can be placed confidently in
God.
1 Peter 1:21 NLT

God is our refuge and strength, an ever-
present help in trouble. Therefore we will not
fear, though the earth give way and the
mountains fall into the heart of the sea.
Psalm 46: 1-2 NIV

The LORD God is a sun and shield; he
bestows favor and honor. No good thing
does the LORD withhold from those who
walk uprightly. O LORD of hosts, happy is
everyone who trusts in you.
Psalm 84:11-12 NRSV

Jesus said, "Don't let your hearts be troubled. Trust in God, and trust in me."
John 14:1 NCV

If you want favor with both God and man, and a reputation for good judgment and common sense, then trust the Lord completely; don't ever trust yourself.
Proverbs 3:4-5 TLB

Truly, in our own hearts we believed we would die. But this happened so we would not trust in ourselves but in God, who raises people from the dead.
2 Corinthians 1:9 NCV

Oh, the joys of those who trust the LORD, who have no confidence in the proud, or in those who worship idols.
Psalm 40:4 NLT

Trust in the LORD, and do good; so shalt thou dwell in the land, and verily thou shalt be fed. Delight thyself also in the LORD; and he shall give thee the desires of thine heart. Commit thy way unto the LORD; trust also in him; and he shall bring it to pass.
Psalm 37:3-5 KJV

Do not be afraid, little flock, for your Father has been pleased to give you the kingdom.
Luke 12:32 NIV

I Am Sufficient

I know what you need before you ask.

My Own,

I see that you often get caught up in the concerns and demands of your daily life, and you don't realize that I am here to take good care of you and provide for all your needs. You think that you alone are responsible for your provision—or that you alone control your destiny. Just remember all that I have done for you already, from creating the air that you breathe to the raw materials that provide a roof over your head.

So, please remember that I delight in providing for you, My child. It gives Me great pleasure to bless you—and I love it when you come to Me! I hate to see you struggle when I have all you could ever want or need. I know what you need even before you do. Come to Me and see that I am sufficient to meet any need you may have.

More than enough,

The Great Provider

The steps of good men are directed by the Lord. He delights in each step they take. If they fall it isn't fatal, for the Lord holds them with his hand.
Psalm 37:23-24 TLB

God is our refuge and strength, a very present help in trouble.
Psalm 46:1 NKJV

He said to me: "It is done. I am the Alpha and the Omega, the Beginning and the End. To him who is thirsty I will give to drink without cost from the spring of the water of life."
Revelation 21:6 NIV

Take delight in the LORD,
and he will give you the desires of your heart.
Psalm 37:4 NRSV

The steadfast of mind You will keep in perfect peace, because he trusts in You. Trust in the LORD forever, for in GOD the LORD, we have an everlasting Rock.
Isaiah 26:3-4 NAS

Blessed is the man who trusts in the LORD, and whose hope is the LORD. For he shall be like a tree planted by the waters, which spreads out its roots by the river, and will not fear when heat comes; but its leaf will be green, and will not be anxious in the year of drought, nor will cease from yielding fruit.
Jeremiah 17:7-8 NKJV

My Protective Arms

Throughout the day and night—I am watching over you.

Dear One,

Consider how an earthly father longs to protect his beloved child. How much more do I desire to keep you safe from all harm! My eyes are constantly upon you, twenty-four hours a day! And I even send My angels to render help from time to time.

But more than anything else, I desire to protect your heart and your spirit. For as you know, all earthly bodies will pass away. But the rest of you (the most important part of you) longs to live forever with Me. And that is why I watch over you so diligently. That is why I wrap My everlasting arms of protection and love all around you, and that is why I draw you to Myself. So come to Me and rest in My protection, for you are safe in My arms.

Protected by Me,

The Lord God Almighty

He orders his angels to protect you wherever you go. They will steady you with their hands to keep you from stumbling against the rocks on the trail. You can safely meet a lion or step on poisonous snakes, yes, even trample them beneath your feet!
Psalm 91:11-13 TLB

I will be with you, and I will protect you wherever you go. I will someday bring you safely back to this land. I will be with you constantly until I have finished giving you everything I have promised.
Genesis 28:15 NLT

I will ransom them from the power of the grave; I will redeem them from death. Where, O death, are your plagues? Where, O grave, is your destruction?
Hosea 13:14 NIV

A father of the fatherless and a judge for the widows, is God in His holy habitation.
Psalm 68:5 NAS

I will both lay me down in peace, and sleep: for thou, LORD, only makest me dwell in safety.
Psalm 4:8 KJV

He who dwells in the shelter of the Most High will rest in the shadow of the Almighty.
Psalm 91:1 NIV

Protection

The Lord is faithful and will give you
strength and will protect you from
the Evil One.
2 Thessalonians 3:3 NCV

This is what the LORD says:
"At the right time I will hear your prayers.
On the day of salvation I will help you.
I will protect you,
and you will be the sign of my agreement
with the people.
You will bring back the people to the land
and give the land that is now ruined back
to its owners."
Isaiah 49:8 NCV

My people will dwell in a peaceful
habitation, in secure dwellings, and in
quiet resting places.
Isaiah 32:18 NKJV

He alone is my rock and my salvation, my
fortress; I shall never be shaken.
Psalm 62:2 NRSV

The LORD will protect you from all evil;
He will keep your soul.
The LORD will guard your going out
and your coming in
From this time forth and forever.
Psalm 121:7-8 NAS

The LORD says, "I will rescue
those who love me.
I will protect those who trust in my name.
When they call on me, I will answer;
I will be with them in trouble.
I will rescue them and honor them.
I will satisfy them with a long life
and give them my salvation."
Psalm 91:14-16 NLT

The righteous cry, and the LORD heareth,
and delivereth them out of all
their troubles.
Psalm 34:17 KJV

Then they cried out to the LORD in their
trouble, and He delivered them out
of their distresses.
Psalm 107:6 NKJV

The angel of the LORD encamps around
those who fear him, and he delivers them.
Psalm 34:7 NIV

All Your Needs

*I know the inner stirrings
of your soul.*

Dearly Loved One,

Deep longings stir within you—some you can't quite identify, although you know they exist. And others lie dormant within, waiting for you to discover them. I know all about these things, My child. For I created you with qualities like curiosity and creativity. To deny these desires of the heart would be to live a life that is less than whole, less than fulfilling.

So how do you begin to assess your heart? And how, you ask, can you ever understand such hidden things? It is very simple, dear one; just come to Me. For I alone hold the key that unlocks these doors. I have already set a plan in place to help you discover and fulfill these desires. So, come and ask Me for My wisdom and understanding. And then listen carefully and expectantly. I will show you how to satisfy your hungry heart.

With all glory,

The King of Hearts

☙❧

Delight yourself also in the LORD,
And He shall give you the desires of
your heart.
Psalm 37:4 NKJV

Seek first his kingdom and his righteousness, and all these things will be given to you as well.
Matthew 6:33 NIV

Why are you in despair, O my soul?
And why have you become disturbed
within me?
Hope in God, for I shall again praise Him
For the help of His presence.
Psalm 42:5 NAS

If you want to know what God wants you
to do, ask him, and he will gladly tell you,
for he is always ready to give a bountiful
supply of wisdom to all who ask him; he
will not resent it.
James 1:5 TLB

He fulfills the desires of those who fear
him; he hears their cry and saves them.
Psalm 145:19 NIV

O LORD, you will hear the desire
of the meek.
Psalm 10:17 NRSV

God's Provision

"Do not be afraid; I will provide for you
and your little ones." So he comforted
them and spoke kindly to them.
Genesis 50:21 NAS

Take delight in the LORD,
and he will give you the desires of your
heart.
Psalm 37:4 NRSV

I will provide for you there, because five
years of famine are still to come.
Otherwise you and your household and all
who belong to you will become destitute.
Genesis 45:11 NIV

You are my hiding place;
You preserve me from trouble;
You surround me with songs of
deliverance.
Psalm 32:7 NAS

I led them with cords of human kindness,
with ties of love; I lifted the yoke from
their neck and bent down to feed them.
Hosea 11:4 NIV

*All mankind scratches for its daily
bread, but your heavenly Father knows
your needs.*
Luke 12:30 TLB

At that time you won't need to ask me for
anything, for you can go directly to the
Father and ask him, and he will give you
what you ask for because you use
my name.
John 16:23 TLB

I am with you and will protect you
everywhere you go and will bring you
back to this land. I will not leave you until
I have done what I have promised you.
Genesis 28:15 NCV

Why be like the pagans who are so deeply
concerned about these things?
Your heavenly Father already knows all
your needs.
Matthew 6:32 NLT

Because he has set his love upon Me,
therefore I will deliver him; I will set him
on high, because he has known My name.
He shall call upon Me, and I will answer
him; I will be with him in trouble; I will
deliver him and honor him.
Psalm 91:14-15 NKJV

My Seeds of Faith

Faith is a gift.

Dear Precious One,

Sometimes you think you must "muster" up your own faith, or you place your faith in someone or something that will only disappoint you. I want you to know that faith is simply a gift from Me. Certainly, you must choose to believe and receive it—but I am the One who plants the seed of faith in each heart.

Like other seeds, faith grows slowly and quietly in some hearts and bursts forth with great joy in others. It all depends on how fertile the soil is. But be assured, I have planted it in the darkened depths of your heart, where it will rest until the germ of life begins to grow—miraculously! And all you must do is watch over this seed—nurture and protect it—for I am the One who causes it to flourish. So, you see, faith—like a seed—is a rather simple thing, yet it contains one of the greatest mysteries known to man.

Faithfully yours,

The Lord God

We are sure of this, that he will listen to us whenever we ask him for anything in line with his will. And if we really know he is listening when we talk to him and make our requests, then we can be sure that he will answer us.

1 John 5:14-15 TLB

He replied, "Because you have so little faith. I tell you the truth, if you have faith as small as a mustard seed, you can say to this mountain, 'Move from here to there' and it will move. Nothing will be impossible for you.
Matthew 17:20 NIV

By continuing to have faith you will save
your lives.
Luke 21:19 NCV

"Have faith in God," Jesus answered.
Mark 11:22 NIV

Those who wait for the Lord
will gain new strength;
they will mount up with wings
like eagles,
they will run and not get tired,
they will walk and not become weary.
Isaiah 40:31 NAS

May your unfailing love rest upon us, O
LORD, even as we put our hope in you.
Psalm 33:22 NIV

Come to Me

Tell Me everything, My child. I am waiting.

Dear Beloved One,

When I urge you to come to Me, I simply mean for you to pray, to bring your problems and concerns to Me. Simply finding time to do that can be difficult in your fast-paced world. The best thing is to find the time of day that is most inspiring for you. Is that the quiet morning before your day begins? Is it the still of night before you doze off into restful slumber?

For Me, it is anytime and all the time! For I am always here, waiting for you, always ready to listen. Do you know how much I delight in hearing your voice? What father doesn't enjoy his child's voice? And there is absolutely nothing you can bring that is too small to interest Me. And nothing in your life is so big that it will overwhelm Me. All you say and think is important to Me. So, I encourage you to come to Me throughout the day. Talk to Me while you're driving, sitting, walking, kneeling. I invite you, dear one; come to Me and tell Me what's on your heart.

Listening,

Your Heavenly Father

The prayer of faith will save the sick, and the Lord will raise him up. And if he has committed sins, he will be forgiven.
James 5:15 NKJV

I say to you, whatever things you ask when you pray, believe that you receive them, and you will have them.

Mark 11:24 NKJV

Now about prayer. When you pray, don't be like the hypocrites who love to pray publicly on street corners and in the synagogues where everyone can see them. I assure you, that is all the reward they will ever get. But when you pray, go away by yourself, shut the door behind you, and pray to your Father secretly. Then your Father, who knows all secrets, will reward you.

Matthew 6:5-6 NLT

If my people who are called by My name humble themselves, pray, seek my face, and turn from their wicked ways, then I will hear from heaven, and will forgive their sin and heal their land.

2 Chronicles 7:14 NRSV

The earnest prayer of a righteous man has great power and wonderful results.

James 5:16 TLB

Prayer

Pray to the LORD for the city where you are living, because if good things happen in the city, good things will happen to you also.

Jeremiah 29:7 NCV

The Spirit helps us in our weakness; for we do not know how to pray as we ought, but that very Spirit intercedes with sighs too deep for words.

Romans 8:26 NRSV

He said to them, "When you pray, say:
Our Father in heaven,
Hallowed be Your name.
Your kingdom come.
Your will be done
On earth as it is in heaven.
Give us day by day our daily bread.
And forgive us our sins,
For we also forgive everyone who is indebted to us.
And do not lead us into temptation,
But deliver us from the evil one."

Luke 11:2-4 NKJV

Be still, and know that I am God.
Psalm 46:10 NKJV

For this reason, all who obey you
should pray to you while they still can.
When troubles rise like a flood,
they will not reach them.
Psalm 32:6 NCV

What should I do then? I will pray with
the spirit, but I will pray with the mind
also; I will sing praise with the spirit, but I
will sing praise with the mind also.
1 Corinthians 14:15 NRSV

Devote yourselves to prayer, being
watchful and thankful.
Colossians 4:2 NIV

Pray in the Spirit at all times in every
prayer and supplication. To that end keep
alert and always persevere in supplication
for all the saints.
Ephesians 6:18 NRSV

Then you will call upon Me and go and
pray to Me, and I will listen to you.
Jeremiah 29:12 NKJV

Brothers and Sisters

Spend time with those who also love Me.

Dear Child,

When you invite Me into your life, you become a member of a great family—the family of faith. These sisters and brothers are not perfect; they often fail, and I see the many ways they hurt one another. But nonetheless, they are Mine, and I am at work in their hearts. And part of My work can be accomplished only through you. I need you to join with them and to participate in the process of being changed. For I made you unique and special, and no one else can bring what you bring to the group.

And as My family of faith comes together, exchanging ideas, praying for one another, and forgiving each other, they all become better people. That pleases Me. So, get to know those who are following Me and see what a fulfilling and pleasant experience it can be!

In unity,

The Father of All

Two are better than one,
Because they have a good reward
for their labor.
Ecclesiastes 4:9 NKJV

Make my joy complete by being like-minded, having the same love, being one in spirit and purpose.
Philippians 2:2 NIV

Behold, how good and how pleasant it is
For brothers to dwell together in unity!
Psalm 133:1 NAS

If we live in the light, as God is in the
light, we can share fellowship with each
other. Then the blood of Jesus, God's Son,
cleanses us from every sin.
1 John 1:7 NCV

A true friend is always loyal, and a
brother is born to help in time of need.
Proverbs 17:17 TLB

Love one another with mutual affection;
outdo one another in showing honor.
Romans 12:10 NRSV

Where two or three are gathered in my
name, I am there among them.
Matthew 18:20 NRSV

Fellowship

I am a friend to all who fear you,
to all who follow your precepts.
Psalm 119:63 NIV

They were continually devoting themselves
to the apostles' teaching and to fellowship,
to the breaking of bread and to prayer.
Acts 2:42 NAS

Do not let loyalty and faithfulness forsake
you; bind them around your neck,
write them on the tablet of your heart.
Proverbs 3:3 NRSV

We proclaim to you what we have seen
and heard, so that you also may have
fellowship with us. And our fellowship is
with the Father and with his Son,
Jesus Christ.
1 John 1:3 NIV

Iron sharpens iron, so one man
sharpens another.
Proverbs 27:17 NAS

What fellowship has righteousness with lawlessness? And what communion has light with darkness?
2 Corinthians 6:14 NKJV

They have told the church here of your friendship and your loving deeds. You do well to send them on their way in a manner that pleases God.
3 John 1:6 NLT

It is harder to win back the friendship of an offended brother than to capture a fortified city. His anger shuts you out like iron bars.
Proverbs 18:19 TLB

My loyalty and love will be with him. Through me he will be strong.
Psalm 89:24 NCV

Behold, how good and how pleasant it is for brethren to dwell together in unity!
Psalm 133:1 KJV

A friend loves at all times,
And a brother is born for adversity.
Proverbs 17:17 NKJV

In His Image

*Let Me change you into
My image.*

Dear Child of Mine,

Daily, you are bombarded with the images and ideals of today's culture. Some are good and some are not. And occasionally the negative ones appear so subtly you hardly notice. At other times, they can blast you right in the face. But I want you to understand that this culture's values are not necessarily My values, and even the ways people esteem things like beauty and success can differ greatly from My ways.

So, I invite you to allow Me to mold you into My image. Let Me teach you what is real success (quiet things like serving others and obeying Me). And let Me reveal to you what true beauty is (gentle things like kind deeds and generous hearts). For as you learn to see life through My eyes, your spirit will be lightened, and your life will take on new meaning.

Transforming you,

The King of Kings

Do not conform any longer to the pattern of this world, but be transformed by the renewing of your mind. Then you will be able to test and approve what God's will is—his good, pleasing and perfect will.

Romans 12:2 NIV

If anyone is in Christ, he is a new creation; the old has gone, the new has come!
2 Corinthians 5:17 NIV

Jesus looked at them and said, "With men it is impossible, but not with God; for with God all things are possible."
Mark 10:27 NKJV

We are His workmanship, created in Christ Jesus for good works, which God prepared beforehand that we should walk in them.
Ephesians 2:10 NKJV

We, who with unveiled faces all reflect the Lord's glory, are being transformed into his likeness with ever-increasing glory, which comes from the Lord, who is the Spirit.
2 Corinthians 3:18 NIV

The path of the righteous is like the light of dawn, which shines brighter and brighter until full day.
Proverbs 4:18 NRSV

Follow Me

You are My disciple.

Dear One,

To be My disciple, you must learn to follow Me. Now, I know this generation greatly respects leaders and doesn't admire followers very much, but before one aspires to lead, he does well to first learn to follow. And it isn't difficult to follow Me; for I don't place great hardships upon you, and I desire to help you every step of the way.

There are several steps that will help you follow Me. First, you'll want to spend time with Me, to get better acquainted with the way I do things. Next, you'll want to learn to recognize My voice, so you'll know what I want you to do. And finally, I need you to do what I ask, knowing that it is for your own good. So, you see, to follow Me is really quite simple.

Leading the way,

The Lord of Lords

The LORD disciplines those he loves,
as a father the son he delights in.
Proverbs 3:12 NIV

You should realize that just as a parent disciplines a child, the LORD your God disciplines you to help you.
Deuteronomy 8:5 NLT

Jesus said to His disciples, "If anyone wishes to come after Me, he must deny himself, and take up his cross and follow Me."
Matthew 16:24 NAS

He will teach the ways that are right and best to those who humbly turn to him.
Psalm 25:9 TLB

They disciplined us for a short time as seemed best to them, but He disciplines us for our good, so that we may share His holiness.
Hebrews 12:10 NAS

I am the one who corrects and disciplines everyone I love. Be diligent and turn from your indifference.
Revelation 3:19 NLT

Let My Light Shine in You

You are My lamp to a darkened world.

Dear One,

Do you know that I want to shine right through you? Do you know how that happens? You see, I am the light of the world. My truth, My love, My grace can shine like a beacon into your life. And if you allow Me, I can flow from you to those around you.

But don't be worried, my friend, for this phenomenon does not depend upon your own strength or power. You are only the lamp—the vessel. I am the one who provides the energy to create the light. All I need from you is a willingness to be used to help others see the light of My love for them. So let My light flow through you—and then witness firsthand how My love and truth and grace can chase away the darkness!

With no shadows,

The Light of the World

∞

The LORD is my light and my salvation;
whom shall I fear?
Psalm 27:1 KJV

O Lord, you are my light!
You make my darkness bright.
2 Samuel 22:29 TLB

If we walk in the Light as He Himself is in
the Light, we have fellowship with one
another, and the blood of Jesus His Son
cleanses us from all sin.
1 John 1:7 NAS

You are the light of the world. A city on a
hill cannot be hidden. Neither do people
light a lamp and put it under a bowl.
Instead they put it on its stand, and it
gives light to everyone in the house. In the
same way, let your light shine before men,
that they may see your good deeds and
praise your Father in heaven.
Matthew 5:14-16 NIV

God is at work within you, helping you
want to obey him, and then helping you
do what he wants.
Philippians 2:13 TLB

Your Place in My World

I have special plans for you.

Dear Beloved,

Sometimes you feel like you don't fit in this world. Perhaps that's because you do not yet realize why you were placed here on the earth, for what reason you were created. I want you to know that there is a very special purpose for your life. And if you allow Me, I will reveal my earthly plans for you—one step at a time.

For your life is unlike any other, and you can touch certain people in ways that no one else can. You are strategically positioned to reach out to others. And I hope you will show My love, My grace, My forgiveness to those along your path. Trust Me and allow Me to continue My work within you. Learn to hear that quiet voice within as, day by day, I lead you through your life. And never forget that you're where you are for a very good reason.

In infinite wisdom,

The Lord of All

He who has found his life will lose it, and
he who has lost his life for My sake
will find it.
Matthew 10:39 NAS

Commit your works to the LORD,
And your thoughts will be established.
Proverbs 16:3 NKJV

We have not ceased praying for you and
asking that you may be filled with the
knowledge of God's will in all spiritual
wisdom and understanding.
Colossians 1:9 NRSV

It is God's will that your good lives should
silence those who make foolish
accusations against you.
1 Peter 2:15 NLT

Help me to do your will, for you are my
God. Lead me in good paths, for your
Spirit is good.
Psalm 143:10 TLB

He who searches our hearts knows the
mind of the Spirit, because the Spirit
intercedes for the saints in accordance
with God's will.
Romans 8:27 NIV

59

The Plan

Patient endurance is what you need now, so
you will continue to do God's will. Then you
will receive all that he has promised.
Hebrews 10:36 NLT

You are free from the law, but that doesn't
mean you are free to do wrong. Live as those
who are free to do only God's will at all times.
1 Peter 2:16 TLB

Lead me in the path of your commands,
because that makes me happy.
Psalm 119:35 NCV

Who knows whether you have come to the
kingdom for such a time as this?
Esther 4:14 NKJV

Do not conform any longer to the pattern of
this world, but be transformed by the
renewing of your mind. Then you will be able
to test and approve what God's will is—his
good, pleasing and perfect will.
Romans 12:2 NIV

Anyone who does God's will is my
brother, and my sister, and my mother.
Mark 3:35 TLB

When the Spirit of truth comes, he will lead
you into all truth. He will not speak his
own words, but he will speak only what he
hears, and he will tell you what is to come.
John 16:13 NCV

If anyone chooses to do God's will, he will
find out whether my teaching comes from
God or whether I speak on my own.
John 7:17 NIV

I have come down from heaven not to do
my will but to do the will of him
who sent me.
John 6:38 NIV

You ought to say, "If the Lord wishes, we
will live and do this or that."
James 4:15 NRSV

The world is passing away, and the
lust of it; but he who does the will
of God abides forever.
1 John 2:17 NKJV

Your Heart, Soul, Mind

Love Me completely.

Dear One Whom I Love,

I have written of My great love for you—it is vast, never ending, and unconditional. But what of your love for Me?

I want you to love Me with all of your heart—that innermost part of your being, the quiet place where your spirit dwells. And I desire for you to love Me with all of your soul—the part of you that laughs and cries and understands beauty. I want you to love Me with all your mind—with all of your wisdom and intellect. And finally I want you to love Me with every ounce of your strength—to pour yourself out for Me, knowing that I will renew you again.

I ask for such a complete and sacrificial love because I know that when you love Me with all your heart, you will listen to My words and follow as I lead you. This will help you to make good choices—choices that will bring happiness, fulfillment, and success to your life. I want you to love Me so that I can help you deal with your problems and enjoy your blessings. I want you to love Me so that you will better know My love for you.

In total love,

Your Heavenly Father

∽∾

Don't just pretend that you love others.
Really love them. Hate what is wrong.
Stand on the side of the good.
Romans 12:9 NLT

He who has My commandments and keeps them, it is he who loves Me. And he who loves Me will be loved by My Father, and I will love him and manifest Myself to him.
John 14:21 NKJV

"'Love the Lord your God with all your heart and with all your soul and with all your mind and with all your strength.' The second is this: 'Love your neighbor as yourself.' There is no commandment greater than these."

"Well said, teacher," the man replied. "You are right in saying that God is one and there is no other but him. To love him with all your heart, with all your understanding and with all your strength, and to love your neighbor as yourself is more important than all burnt offerings and sacrifices."
Mark 12:30-33 NIV

With Jesus' help we will continually offer our sacrifice of praise to God by telling others of the glory of his name.
Hebrews 13:15 TLB

Loving God

May the Lord make your love grow more
and multiply for each other and for all
people so that you will love others
as we love you.

1 Thessalonians 3:12 NCV

If I had the gift of being able to speak in
other languages without learning them, and
could speak in every language there is in all
of heaven and earth, but didn't love others,
I would only be making noise. If I had the
gift of prophecy and knew all about what is
going to happen in the future, knew
everything about everything, but didn't love
others, what good would it do? Even if I
had the gift of faith so that I could speak to
a mountain and make it move, I would still
be worth nothing at all without love.

1 Corinthians 13:1-2 TLB

He said to him, "You shall love the Lord
your God with all your heart, and with all
your soul, and with all your mind."

Matthew 22:37 NRSV

If I gave everything I have to poor people, and if I were burned alive for preaching the Gospel but didn't love others, it would be of no value whatever.
1 Corinthians 13:3 TLB

The second command is like the first:
"Love your neighbor as you love
yourself." All the law and the writings
of the prophets depend on these
two commands.
Matthew 22:39 NCV

I know it is far more important to love
him with all my heart and understanding
and strength, and to love others as myself,
than to offer all kinds of sacrifices on the
altar of the Temple.
Mark 12:33 TLB

Because he has set his love upon Me,
therefore I will deliver him; I will set him
on high, because he has known My name.
Psalm 91:14 NKJV

Jesus answered him, "If a man loves me,
he will keep my word, and my Father will
love him, and we will come to him and
make our home with him."
John 14:23 NRSV

Love Yourself

Forgiveness and acceptance start here.

Dear Loved One,

You can be so hard on yourself sometimes. So unforgiving, so judgmental, so harsh. You see yourself in a contorted mirror, but it's not how I see you, not at all! I want you to begin to look at yourself differently—through My eyes. And I want you to forgive yourself. First of all, forgive yourself for not being perfect, for making mistakes, and for being human. Then admit where you've blown it and forgive yourself all over again.

Next, begin to accept yourself in the same way that I accept you—with mercy, grace, and love. See that you were created in My image so you are unique and infinitely valuable. Finally, choose to love yourself—for I love you. Jesus said, "Love your neighbor as you love yourself." He understood that no one can love another properly until he loves himself.

In perfect love,

Your Father in Heaven

If, however, you are fulfilling the royal law according to the Scripture, "YOU SHALL LOVE YOUR NEIGHBOR AS YOURSELF," you are doing well.
James 2:8 NAS

Don't seek vengeance. Don't bear a grudge; but love your neighbor as yourself, for I am Jehovah.
Leviticus 19:18 TLB

You should know that your body is a
temple for the Holy Spirit who is in you.
You have received the Holy Spirit from
God. So you do not belong to yourselves.
1 Corinthians 6:19 NCV

Are not two sparrows sold for a copper
coin? And not one of them falls to the
ground apart from your Father's will. But
the very hairs of your head are all
numbered. Do not fear therefore; you are
of more value than many sparrows.
Matthew 10:29-31 NKJV

You created my inmost being; you knit me
together in my mother's womb. I praise
you because I am fearfully and
wonderfully made; your works are
wonderful, I know that full well.
Psalm 139:13-14 NIV

Love as I Love

Love those around you with My love.

Dear Child of Mine,

There will always be those people in this world who seem somewhat unlovable. So it has been since the beginning of time. But be thankful for them. For they're like an invitation for you to come to Me and to allow Me to love through you. When someone is good and kind and easy to love, you don't need My help. But when someone is cantankerous and moody, it requires more of you—it requires Me. And when you involve Me, we can begin to make a difference. My love combined with your love is a miracle waiting to happen.

Learn to let Me love through you. And be reminded that My love isn't an ordinary kind of love—it's unconditional, unending, and full of grace. As you practice loving others in this fashion, just watch and see how it changes your own heart, too!

Most lovingly,

The Lord on High

⬯⬯

God so loved the world that He gave His only begotten Son, that whoever believes in Him should not perish but have everlasting life.
John 3:16 NKJV

Give thanks to the LORD because
he is good.
His love continues forever.
Give thanks to the God of gods.
His love continues forever.
Give thanks to the Lord of lords.
His love continues forever.
Psalm 136:1-3 NCV

Live in such a way that God's love can
bless you as you wait for the eternal life
that our Lord Jesus Christ in his mercy is
going to give you. Show mercy to those
whose faith is wavering.
Jude 21-22 NLT

Beloved, let us love one another, for love
is from God; and everyone who loves is
born of God and knows God.
1 John 4:7 NAS

Forgive as I Forgive

Follow My example in forgiving others.

Dear Forgiven One,

Have you ever noticed how a healthy pond both receives and gives fresh water? That constant come-and-go current keeps the water clean and pure. And so it is with forgiveness, dear friend. In the same way that I pour My forgiveness onto you, I want you to freely and generously pour it onto all those around you.

So I encourage you to forgive quickly. The moment you realize you've been wronged, step away from bitterness and move toward forgiveness. Don't wait for offenders to ask, just quietly forgive them and move on. And like that pond full of crystal-clear water, you, too, will be filled with life, health, and happiness.

In mercy and grace,

The One Who Forgave All

This is how my heavenly Father will treat
each of you unless you forgive your
brother from your heart.
Matthew 18:35 NIV

The discretion of a man makes him slow to anger, And his glory is to overlook a transgression.
Proverbs 19:11 NKJV

Since you have been chosen by God who has given you this new kind of life, and because of his deep love and concern for you, you should practice tenderhearted mercy and kindness to others. Don't worry about making a good impression on them but be ready to suffer quietly and patiently.
Colossians 3:12 TLB

If we confess our sins to him, he can be depended on to forgive us and to cleanse us from every wrong. [And it is perfectly proper for God to do this for us because Christ died to wash away our sins.]
1 John 1:9 TLB

Be ye kind one to another, tenderhearted, forgiving one another, even as God for Christ's sake hath forgiven you.
Ephesians 4:32 KJV

Forgiveness

By grace you have been saved through faith; and that not of yourselves, it is the gift of God; not as a result of works, so that no one may boast.

Ephesians 2:8-9 NAS

Your heavenly Father will forgive you if you forgive those who sin against you; but if you refuse to forgive them, he will not forgive you.

Matthew 6:14-15 TLB

God demonstrates his own love for us in this: While we were still sinners, Christ died for us.

Romans 5:8 NIV

If anyone has caused grief, he has not so much grieved me as he has grieved all of you, to some extent—not to put it too severely. The punishment inflicted on him by the majority is sufficient for him. Now instead, you ought to forgive and comfort him, so that he will not be overwhelmed by excessive sorrow.

2 Corinthians 2:5-7 NIV

In him we have redemption through his blood, the forgiveness of our trespasses, according to the riches of his grace.
Ephesians 1:7 NRSV

I wrote to you as I did to find out how far you would go in obeying me. When you forgive this man, I forgive him, too. And when I forgive him (for whatever is to be forgiven), I do so with Christ's authority for your benefit, so that Satan will not outsmart us. For we are very familiar with his evil schemes.
2 Corinthians 2:9-11 NLT

Bearing with one another, and forgiving each other, whoever has a complaint against anyone; just as the Lord forgave you, so also should you.
Colossians 3:13 NAS

Whenever you stand praying, forgive, if you have anything against anyone; so that your Father in heaven may also forgive you your trespasses.
Mark 11:25 NRSV

He that covereth a transgression seeketh love; but he that repeateth a matter separateth very friends.
Proverbs 17:9 KJV

Don't Judge My Children

When you look down on another, you look down on Me.

Dear Precious One,

How does an artist feel when someone criticizes his workmanship? Of course, he takes it personally—after all, his art is an extension of himself. And so it is with Me. I don't like to hear people judging and criticizing others. Not only did I create each person, but I created him or her in My own image. When I hear someone being criticized, I take it personally.

You see, I know all the struggles My children are facing. You may see some of those, but I'm the only one who knows the whole story. I look at all My children with eyes of love and understanding. You will never see other people the way I see them, and they will never see you the way I do. But I hope that you will place your confidence in Me and know that I am at work. And then show My mercy and love to those around you!

Knowing all,

The Lord God Almighty

There is neither Jew nor Greek, slave nor free,
male nor female, for you are all one
in Christ Jesus.
Galatians 3:28 NIV

Stop judging others, and you will not be judged. Stop criticizing others, or it will all come back on you. If you forgive others, you will be forgiven.

Luke 6:37 NLT

The LORD does not look at the things man looks at. Man looks at the outward appearance, but the LORD looks at the heart.
1 Samuel 16:7 NIV

My brothers, as believers in our glorious Lord Jesus Christ, don't show favoritism.
James 2:1 NIV

Finally, all of you be of one mind, having compassion for one another; love as brothers, be tenderhearted, be courteous; not returning evil for evil or reviling for reviling, but on the contrary blessing, knowing that you were called to this, that you may inherit a blessing.
1 Peter 3:8-9 NKJV

Be kind to one another, tenderhearted, forgiving one another, even as God in Christ forgave you.
Ephesians 4:32 NKJV

I Made You Just Right

You were created with designer DNA.

Dear One,

Even before your mother was aware of your presence, I knew all about you. I carefully arranged your genes to make you just as you are. And I think you turned out just right! Now, I know you question my workmanship from time to time—probably due to the influence of the culture in which you live. But know this, I am very pleased with My creation!

When you feel the urge to criticize yourself, I want you to look more deeply, and with a thankful heart, consider the gifts and abilities I have given you. Then consider whether or not you fully utilize all those gifts. And finally, come to Me and ask Me to help you to become all that I have planned for you to be. For you cannot even imagine what joys that might bring!

With mighty plans,

Your Creator

The Lord will work out his plans for my life—for your lovingkindness, Lord, continues forever. Don't abandon me—for you made me.
Psalm 138:8 TLB

*Remember now your Creator in the days
of your youth.
Ecclesiastes 12:1 NKJV*

You created my inmost being;
you knit me together
in my mother's womb.
I praise you because I am fearfully and
wonderfully made;
your works are wonderful,
I know that full well.
Psalm 139:13-14 NIV

God's ways are as hard to discern as the
pathways of the wind, and as mysterious
as a tiny baby being formed
in a mother's womb.
Ecclesiastes 11:5 NLT

God created man in His own image, in the
image of God He created him; male and
female He created them.
Genesis 1:27 NAS

God's Design

We are His workmanship, created in
Christ Jesus for good works, which God
prepared beforehand that we
should walk in them.
Ephesians 2:10 NKJV

By You I have been sustained
from my birth;
You are He who took me from my
mother's womb;
My praise is continually of You.
Psalm 71:6 NAS

It is I who made the earth, and created
man upon it.
I stretched out the heavens with My hands
And I ordained all their host.
Isaiah 45:12 NAS

Can a mother forget the baby at her breast
and have no compassion on the child she
has borne? Though she may forget, I will
not forget you! See, I have engraved you
on the palms of my hands; your walls are
ever before me.
Isaiah 49:15-16 NIV

I will be your God throughout your lifetime—until your hair is white with age. I made you, and I will care for you. I will carry you along and save you.
Isaiah 46:4 NLT

Take a look at the hippopotamus! I made
him, too, just as I made you!
Job 40:15 TLB

Ask now concerning the former days
which were before you, since the day that
God created man on the earth, and inquire
from one end of the heavens to the other.
Has anything been done like this great
thing, or has anything been heard like it?
Deuteronomy 4:32 NAS

Know that the LORD Himself is God;
It is He who has made us,
and not we ourselves;
We are His people and the
sheep of His pasture.
Psalm 100:3 NAS

The Lord appeared to him from far away.
I have loved you with an everlasting love;
therefore I have continued
my faithfulness to you.
Jeremiah 31:3 NRSV

My Earthen Vessels

*All I ask is that you stay
in My hand.*

Dear Work of My Hands,

Sometimes you look at your life and all you see are the imperfections. And it's true, being human, you can't escape them. But I don't expect your life to run perfectly, and I know you still have challenges in your future. All I ask is that you trust Me and allow Me to use you just as you are. For I have created you to be a vessel, an earthen vessel, filled with Me.

To be My vessel you don't need to be perfect— just available. Consider a man perishing from thirst. At the well, he finds an old, chipped piece of pottery in the form of a serviceable jug. Perhaps he knows of a finely glazed ceramic pitcher on the other side of town. But the stoneware jug is here right now, ready to be used. For which vessel would he be most thankful? So, I remind you, trust Me, and remain available to Me. Let Me use you to pour out My love upon others. And in due time, your earthen imperfections will be transformed into heavenly glories!

In My hands,

Your King

Now, O LORD, You are our Father,
We are the clay, and You our potter;
And all of us are the work of Your hand.
Isaiah 64:8 NAS

God made me in my mother's womb, and he also made them; the same God formed both of us in our mothers' wombs.
Job 31:15 NCV

He said to me, "My grace is sufficient for you, for power is made perfect in weakness." So, I will boast all the more gladly of my weaknesses, so that the power of Christ may dwell in me.
2 Corinthians 12:9 NRSV

Blessed is the man who trusts in the LORD, whose confidence is in him. He will be like a tree planted by the water that sends out its roots by the stream. It does not fear when heat comes; its leaves are always green. It has no worries in a year of drought and never fails to bear fruit.
Jeremiah 17:7-8 NIV

Then he said to me, "This is the word of the LORD to Zerubbabel saying, 'Not by might nor by power, but by My Spirit,' says the LORD of hosts."
Zechariah 4:6 NAS

True Perfection

Woe to you who strive with your Maker,
earthen vessels with the potter!
Does the clay say to the one who fashions
it, "What are you making"?
or "Your work has no handles"?
Isaiah 45:9 NRSV

I came to you in weakness and fear, and
with much trembling. My message and my
preaching were not with wise and
persuasive words, but with a
demonstration of the Spirit's power, so that
your faith might not rest on men's
wisdom, but on God's power.
1 Corinthians 2:3-5 NIV

His delight is in the law of the LORD, and
on his law he meditates day and night. He
is like a tree planted by streams of water,
that yields its fruit in its season, and its
leaf does not wither. In all that
he does, he prospers.
Psalm 1:2-3 NRSV

We are His workmanship, created in Christ Jesus for good works, which God prepared beforehand that we should walk in them.
Ephesians 2:10 NKJV

We have this treasure in earthen vessels, that the excellence of the power may be of God and not of us. We are hard pressed on every side, yet not crushed; we are perplexed, but not in despair; persecuted, but not forsaken; struck down, but not destroyed—always carrying about in the body the dying of the Lord Jesus, that the life of Jesus also may be manifested in our body. For we who live are always delivered to death for Jesus' sake, that the life of Jesus also may be manifested in our mortal flesh. So then death is working in us, but life in you.
2 Corinthians 4:7-12 NKJV

The foolishness of God is wiser than man's wisdom, and the weakness of God is stronger than man's strength.
1 Corinthians 1:25 NIV

"The LORD is my portion," says my soul, "Therefore I hope in Him!"
Lamentations 3:24 NKJV

Hear My Voice

Learn to listen with attentive ears.

Dear One,

Sometimes you think I'm not talking to you. Perhaps you're rushing through a busy day and you long for help or direction, but you don't think you'll get it, or you're just too distracted to take time to ask. But, I want you to know that if you slow down a little and listen, you will begin to hear My voice because I am eager to speak to you.

Amen

My voice is like the whisper of snow falling in a solitary wood, like the sound of the breeze gently caressing the trees. And to hear Me, you must train your inner ears to listen. Really listen. You must develop and nurture a quiet spirit that is ready to hear. You must tune yourself to My frequency. And that takes patience, time, and a willingness to quiet your heart in My presence. But it is well worth it, for I have wonderful things to tell you.

Whispers of love,

Your Heavenly Father

You will find me when you seek me, if you look for me in earnest.
Jeremiah 29:13 TLB

He who has ears to hear,
let him hear.
Matthew 11:15 NAS

Samuel answered, "What pleases the
LORD more. . . sacrifices
or obedience to his voice?
It is better to obey than to sacrifice.
It is better to listen to God."
1 Samuel 15:22 NCV

I will listen to God the LORD.
He has ordered peace for those who
worship him.
Don't let them go back to foolishness.
Psalm 85:8 NCV

Be careful and do not refuse to listen
when God speaks. Others refused to listen
to him when he warned them on earth,
and they did not escape. So it will be
worse for us if we refuse to listen to God
who warns us from heaven.
Hebrews 12:25 NCV

Know That I Am God

Respect My power and glory and majesty.

My Child,

As much as I long for you to know Me as your heavenly Father, and to have you, like a small child, crawl onto My lap and experience My love, I also want you to understand My incredible omnipotence. For, it is true, I am the Lord God Almighty. I did create the heavens and the earth. And I am the beginning and the end— everything is in My hands. You'll never fully understand My power and majesty. But I want you to respect it.

For only as you respect it can you rest in the assurance that I, the Lord God, have everything under control. And only then can you begin to trust that I hold your life in My hands and I am able to protect you and keep you each day of your life. So experience the glorious awe of knowing who I am, and relish My majesty.

In power and majesty,

The Almighty

After the earthquake a fire, but the LORD
was not in the fire; and after the
fire a still small voice.
1 Kings 19:12 NKJV

Sing for joy to God our strength;
shout aloud to the God of Jacob!
Psalm 81:1 NIV

Jesus has the power of God, by which he
has given us everything we need to live
and to serve God. We have these things
because we know him. Jesus called us by
his glory and goodness.
2 Peter 1:3 NCV

Without faith it is impossible to please
Him, for he who comes to God must
believe that He is, and that He is a
rewarder of those who diligently seek
Him.
Hebrews 11:6 NKJV

Know therefore that the LORD your God
is God; he is the faithful God, keeping his
covenant of love to a thousand
generations of those who love him
and keep his commands.
Deuteronomy 7:9 NIV

All Knowing

So that your faith might not rest on men's
wisdom, but on God's power.
1 Corinthians 2:5 NIV

Though He was crucified in weakness, yet
He lives by the power of God. For we also
are weak in Him, but we shall live with
Him by the power of God toward you.
2 Corinthians 13:4 NKJV

O Lord, my Strength and Fortress, my
Refuge in the day of trouble, nations from
around the world will come to you saying,
"Our fathers have been foolish, for they
have worshiped worthless idols!"
Jeremiah 16:19 TLB

The works of his hands are verity and
judgment; all his commandments are sure.
They stand fast for ever and ever, and are
done in truth and uprightness.
Psalm 111:7-8 KJV

The Sovereign LORD is my strength;
he makes my feet like the feet of a deer,
he enables me to go on the heights.
Habakkuk 3:19 NIV

I said, "I have toiled in vain,
I have spent My strength for nothing and
vanity; yet surely the justice due to Me is
with the LORD,
and My reward with My God."
And now says the LORD, who formed Me
from the womb to be His Servant,
to bring Jacob back to Him, so that Israel
might be gathered to Him
(for I am honored in the sight of the LORD,
and My God is My strength).
Isaiah 49:4-5 NAS

I am not ashamed of the gospel, for it is
the power of God for salvation to
everyone who believes, to the Jew first
and also to the Greek.
Romans 1:16 NAS

I love you, O LORD, my strength.
Psalm 18:1 NIV

Trust Me with Everything

*Put all areas of your life
into My hands.*

Dear Precious One,

I have spoken to you about trusting Me with your heart. And certainly that is no small commitment. But now I encourage you to trust Me with all areas of your life. I know how you like to hang on to certain things—not completely sure that I will take care of them like you would. Things like loved ones, personal goals, dreams, aspirations. Perhaps you fear that if you hand them over to Me, I will take them away from you—remove them altogether. But that isn't the way I work.

I want you to know that I have only your very best interest at heart. And if you trust Me with your life, I can help you accomplish what is truly valuable and important to you. And I believe that's what you really want, too.

Worthy of your trust,

The Lord Who Loves You

He established the clouds above
and fixed securely the
fountains of the deep.
Proverbs 8:28 NIV

We have this assurance: Those who belong to God shall live again. Their bodies shall rise again! Those who dwell in the dust shall awake and sing for joy! For God's light of life will fall like dew upon them!
Isaiah 26:19 TLB

Hear my cry, O God;
listen to my prayer.
From the end of the earth I call to you,
when my heart is faint.
Lead me to the rock
that is higher than I;
for you are my refuge,
a strong tower against the enemy.
Let me abide in your tent forever,
find refuge under the shelter
of your wings.
Psalm 61:1-4 NRSV

Blessed is the man who makes the LORD
his trust, who does not look to the proud,
to those who turn aside to false gods.
Psalm 40:4 NIV

Trusting in God

Thus the LORD GOD, the Holy One of Israel, has said, "In repentance and rest you will be saved, in quietness and trust is your strength."
Isaiah 30:15 NAS

Thus says the Lord GOD, see I am laying in Zion a foundation stone, a tested stone, a precious cornerstone, a sure foundation: "One who trusts will not panic."
Isaiah 28:16 NRSV

Thou wilt keep him in perfect peace, whose mind is stayed on thee: because he trusteth in thee. Trust ye in the LORD for ever: for in the LORD JEHOVAH is everlasting strength.
Isaiah 26:3-4 KJV

Blessed is the man who trusts in the LORD, and whose hope is the LORD. For he shall be like a tree planted by the waters, which spreads out its roots by the river, and will not fear when heat comes; but its leaf will be green, and will not be anxious in the year of drought, nor will cease from yielding fruit.
Jeremiah 17:7-8 NKJV

*Cast your cares on the LORD and he
will sustain you; he will never let the
righteous fall.
Psalm 55:22 NIV*

The LORD loves justice and does not
forsake His godly ones; they are preserved
forever, but the descendants of the wicked
will be cut off.
Psalm 37:28 NAS

Because he cleaves to me in love, I will
deliver him; I will protect him, because he
knows my name. When he calls to me, I
will answer him; I will be with him in
trouble, I will rescue him
and honor him.
Psalm 91:14-15 NRSV

As for God, his way is perfect; the word of
the LORD is tried: he is a buckler to all
them that trust in him.
2 Samuel 22:31 KJV

You are my hiding place;
You shall preserve me from trouble;
You shall surround me
with songs of deliverance.
Psalm 32:7 NKJV

My Joy Shall Abound

*You bring Me great joy
and gladness.*

My Treasure,

Do you have any idea how much joy you bring to My heart? Oh, how I smile when I look upon you and see how you're trying to live your life in a worthy manner. Of course, I know when you blow it—you're still human, aren't you? But just as an earthly father derives pleasure from watching his children meet the challenges of growing up, so I receive great joy and happiness from watching you.

As I've said before, I don't expect perfection from you. And I surely don't enjoy showy performances of "good works." What brings Me the uttermost joy are the simple things—those traits like a sacrificial life, childlike faith, a loving heart, an honest spirit. Those bring Me the greatest delight. And I rejoice as I see these things in you!

Joyfully,

Your Father God

A merry heart does good, like medicine,
But a broken spirit dries the bones.
Proverbs 17:22 NKJV

Let the heavens be glad, the earth rejoice;
let the vastness of the roaring seas
demonstrate his glory. Praise him for the
growing fields, for they display his
greatness. Let the trees of the forest
rustle with praise.
Psalm 96:11-12 TLB

He crowns it all with green, lush pastures
in the wilderness; hillsides blossom with
joy. The pastures are filled with flocks of
sheep, and the valleys are carpeted with
grain. All the world shouts with
joy, and sings.
Psalm 65:11-13 TLB

Even if I am being poured out as a drink
offering upon the sacrifice and service of
your faith, I rejoice and share my joy with
you all. You too, I urge you, rejoice in the
same way and share
your joy with me.
Philippians 2:17-18 NAS

95

Joy

Let your roots grow down into him and
draw up nourishment from him.
See that you go on growing in the Lord,
and become strong and vigorous
in the truth you were taught.
Let your lives overflow with joy and
thanksgiving for all he has done.
Colossians 2:7 TLB

Shout joyfully to the LORD, all the earth;
break forth and sing for
joy and sing praises.
Psalm 98:4 NAS

I delight greatly in the LORD; my soul
rejoices in my God. For he has clothed me
with garments of salvation and arrayed me
in a robe of righteousness, as a bridegroom
adorns his head like a priest, and as a
bride adorns herself with her jewels.
Isaiah 61:10 NIV

The Kingdom of God is not a matter of
what we eat or drink, but of living a life of
goodness and peace and joy
in the Holy Spirit.
Romans 14:17 NLT

Let all who take refuge in you rejoice;
let them sing joyful praises forever.
Protect them,
so all who love your name
may be filled with joy.
Psalm 5:11 NLT

Let the godly ones exult in glory;
Let them sing for joy on their beds.
Psalm 149:5 NAS

The precepts of the LORD are right,
rejoicing the heart;
The commandment of the LORD is pure,
enlightening the eyes.
Psalm 19:8 NAS

You have loved righteousness and hated
wickedness; therefore God, your God, has
anointed you with the oil of gladness
beyond your companions.
Hebrews 1:9 NRSV

Blessed Are the Peacemakers

Calm words are like a soothing balm.

Dear One,

I know how the human heart, when left to its own devices, can thrive on conflict and controversy. This is apparent by the way people gravitate to a fight scene or become easily agitated by a fiery speaker. But these are not My ways. I desire My children to be ruled by peace—My peace. And when you are ruled by My peace, it will flow out of your life and bless others. That's when you become a real peacemaker.

Oh, how I love peacemakers. As you experience My peace, you will begin to understand how you can share words of peace and comfort with others—words that are like a soothing balm. For I can show you how to smooth over a rough situation, and I can help you to calm a distressed heart. Come and let Me teach you My peace, My child.

Shalom,

The God of Love

When a man's ways please the LORD,
He makes even his enemies to be
at peace with him.
Proverbs 16:7 NKJV

We pursue the things which make for
peace and the building up of one another.
Romans 14:19 NAS

Do not accuse a man for no reason—
when he has done you no harm.
Proverbs 3:30 NIV

Christ himself is our way of peace. He has
made peace between us Jews and you
Gentiles by making us all one family,
breaking down the wall of contempt
that used to separate us.
Ephesians 2:14 TLB

I urge that entreaties and prayers,
petitions and thanksgivings, be made
on behalf of all men.
1 Timothy 2:1 NAS

The mind of sinful man is death, but the
mind controlled by the Spirit is
life and peace.
Romans 8:6 NIV

Peace

Do your part to live in peace with everyone,
as much as possible.
Romans 12:18 NLT

Those who love Your law have great peace,
And nothing causes them to stumble.
Psalm 119:165 NAS

The LORD will give strength to His people;
The LORD will bless His people with peace.
Psalm 29:11 NKJV

God is not a God of disorder but of peace.
1 Corinthians 14:33 NIV

He will judge between the nations,
and will render decisions for many peoples;
and they will hammer their swords into
plowshares and their spears into pruning
hooks. Nation will not lift up sword against
nation, and never again will they learn war.
Isaiah 2:4 NAS

I say to you, love your enemies and pray for those who persecute you.
Matthew 5:44 NAS

The fruit of righteousness is sown in peace
by those who make peace.
James 3:18 NKJV

He himself is our peace, who has made the
two one and has destroyed the barrier,
the dividing wall of hostility.
Ephesians 2:14 NIV

Become complete. Be of good comfort, be
of one mind, live in peace; and the God of
love and peace will be with you.
2 Corinthians 13:11 NKJV

I am leaving you with a gift—peace of
mind and heart! And the peace I give isn't
fragile like the peace the world gives. So
don't be troubled or afraid.
John 14:27 TLB

Blessed are the peacemakers,
For they shall be called sons of God.
Matthew 5:9 NKJV

In My Time

*Patience comes
through waiting.*

Dear One,

I know it's hard to wait. Whether it's in a doctor's waiting room while someone you love is in pain or for an important call and the phone refuses to ring. Whether it's due to long lines, inept clerks, or slow elevators, waiting is tough. And the fact is our culture has become accustomed to having what it wants quickly—often at the push of a button—and patience can seem a rare virtue indeed.

I operate on a different time clock than you do. What you may consider a waste of time, I may see as an opportunity for something altogether different. Perhaps when the stoplight is red for a prolonged period, I simply want you to take that moment to bring your cares to Me. Or when someone doesn't show up on time, perhaps you need to quiet your spirit and say a quick prayer for that person's welfare. So, practice patience and remember, My timing is perfect.

Patiently,

The Creator of All Time

A man's wisdom gives him patience; it is to
his glory to overlook an offense.
Proverbs 19:11 NIV

Finishing is better than starting!
Patience is better than pride!
Ecclesiastes 7:8 TLB

Whatever things were written before were
written for our learning, that we through
the patience and comfort of the Scriptures
might have hope. Now may the God of
patience and comfort grant you to be like-
minded toward one another,
according to Christ Jesus.
Romans 15:4-5 NKJV

Patience is better than strength.
Controlling your temper is better
than capturing a city.
Proverbs 16:32 NCV

Rest in the LORD and wait patiently for
Him; do not fret because of him who
prospers in his way, because of the man
who carries out wicked schemes.
Psalm 37:7 NAS

Be Generous, My Child

The best gift is given with a cheerful heart.

Dear Child of Mine,

I know you understand that generosity is a positive attribute. But sometimes you grow overly concerned by your own needs, and it robs the joy of giving to others. So first, My child, come to Me and tell Me what you need. Then trust Me to provide it.

This will make it possible for you to give generously and with a cheerful spirit. For that's the sort of giving that pleases Me most. I delight to see a gift that is given wholeheartedly with no false motives, but simply out of a kind and generous spirit. That's the sort of generosity that I can bless and multiply in unimaginable ways.

The amazing miracle of generosity is that those who gladly share of themselves and their resources always receive far more than the recipients. So, learn to give cheerfully, My child, and watch how I will bless you!

With all generosity,

Your Provider

It is easier for a camel to go through the eye of a needle than for a rich man to enter the kingdom of God.
Matthew 19:24 NIV

As each one has received a gift, minister it to one another, as good stewards of the manifold grace of God.
1 Peter 4:10 NKJV

I needed clothes and you clothed me, I was sick and you looked after me, I was in prison and you came to visit me.
Matthew 25:36 NIV

Let each one give as he purposes in his heart, not grudgingly or of necessity; for God loves a cheerful giver.
2 Corinthians 9:7 NKJV

Blessed are those who are generous, because they feed the poor.
Proverbs 22:9 NLT

Give, and it will be given to you: good measure, pressed down, shaken together, and running over will be put into your bosom. For with the same measure that you use, it will be measured back to you.
Luke 6:38 NKJV

Generosity

Tell them to use their money to do good.
They should be rich in good works and
should give generously to those in need,
always being ready to share with others
whatever God has given them.
1 Timothy 6:18 NLT

You are generous because of your faith.
And I am praying that you will really put
your generosity to work, for in so doing
you will come to an understanding of all
the good things we can do for Christ.
Philemon 6 NLT

Give generously, for your gifts will
return to you later.
Ecclesiastes 11:1 TLB

He will take care of the helpless and poor
when they cry to him; for they have no
one else to defend them.
Psalm 72:12 TLB

A generous person will be enriched, and
one who gives water will get water.
Proverbs 11:25 NRSV

They give generously to those in need.
Their good deeds will never be forgotten.
They will have influence and honor.
Psalm 112:9 NLT

Give generously to him and do so
without a grudging heart; then because of this
the LORD your God will bless you in all your
work and in everything you put your hand to.
Deuteronomy 15:10 NIV

Take care that you do not despise one of
these little ones; for, I tell you, in heaven
their angels continually see the face
of my Father in heaven.
Matthew 18:10 NRSV

In everything I did, I showed you that by this
kind of hard work we must help the weak,
remembering the words the LORD Jesus
himself said: "It is more blessed to give than
to receive."
Acts 20:35 NIV

My Fruit in You

Stay connected to Me.

Dear Beloved,

I know how you desire to grow and mature spiritually. You'd like to be patient and loving and kind on a regular basis—even when times are tough. Yet, I see how you struggle with these qualities, perhaps blaming yourself for not measuring up or being good enough. But there's an easier way, My child. Let Me explain.

Simply abide in Me. Spend time with Me, listen to Me, learn from Me. Let My Spirit lead and guide you. And as a natural result, you will begin to grow and mature without striving. It's like a branch on a fruit tree. As long as that branch remains firmly and healthily attached to the trunk, it cannot help but bear good, wholesome fruit. It's merely a by-product of that intertwined relationship. And so it is with you, dear one; stay connected to Me, and you cannot help but bear spiritual fruit that is both lovely and lasting.

Abundantly,

The Giver of Every Good Gift

When the Holy Spirit controls our lives he will produce this kind of fruit in us: love, joy, peace, patience, kindness, goodness, faithfulness, gentleness and self-control; and here there is no conflict with Jewish laws.

Galatians 5:22-23 TLB

*One who prophesies, preaching the messages
of God, is helping others grow in the Lord,
encouraging and comforting them.*
1 Corinthians 14:3 TLB

Bodily exercise profits a little, but
godliness is profitable for all things,
having promise of the life that now is and
of that which is to come.
1 Timothy 4:8 NKJV

If these things are yours and abound, you
will be neither barren nor unfruitful in the
knowledge of our Lord Jesus Christ.
2 Peter 1:8 NKJV

You did not choose Me but I chose you,
and appointed you that you would go and
bear fruit, and that your fruit would
remain, so that whatever you ask of the
Father in My name He may give to you.
John 15:16 NAS

The fruit of the light consists in all
goodness, righteousness and truth.
Ephesians 5:9 NIV

Reach Out in My Love

Reach out to those around you.

Dear Loved One,

I know it can be overwhelming at times—the world you live in seems so big and so full of people who appear to have little interest in anything beyond getting through another day of life. And the mere idea of reaching out to another person and sharing anything of significance can seem nearly impossible. And then you ask yourself, "What can I possibly say or do that will make any difference to anyone? How can my one little life on this great big planet have any effect at all?"

But that's where I come in, My child. What seems impossible with you is quite possible for Me. And the way I work is one heart at a time—using people just like you to touch lives. So come to Me and ask how we, together, can reach out to someone today. It usually starts out simply—with a smile or quiet act of kindness. But, trust Me, small beginnings can turn into very big things.

Partners in love,

Your Heavenly Father

❧

Preach the Word; be prepared in season
and out of season; correct, rebuke and
encourage—with great patience
and careful instruction.
2 Timothy 4:2 NIV

You love me! You are holding my right hand! You will keep on guiding me all my life with your wisdom and counsel; and afterwards receive me into the glories of heaven!
Psalm 73:23-24 TLB

Dear children, let us not love with words or tongue but with actions and in truth.
1 John 3:18 NIV

When the Holy Spirit has come upon you, you will receive power to testify about me with great effect, to the people in Jerusalem, throughout Judea, in Samaria, and to the ends of the earth, about my death and resurrection.
Acts 1:8 TLB

In everything set them an example by doing what is good. In your teaching show integrity, seriousness and soundness of speech that cannot be condemned, so that those who oppose you may be ashamed because they have nothing bad to say about us.
Titus 2:7-8 NIV

Let Me Touch Your Heart

Healing flows from My hands.

Dear One,

I know your heart, My child, even better than you do. I know about each time you've been hurt; for I witnessed each wound as it occurred, and I can see every scar. Through the years, I have healed many of your wounds, but some remain—still tender to the touch. I want to heal those wounds for you, too. But first you must acknowledge that they exist and bring them to Me. That's when the healing begins.

But keep in mind, My healing is not always instantaneous. It can take days, weeks, even years sometimes. And frequently I use other people to partner with Me in the healing process. So don't be afraid to go to someone you trust with this. For we can all work together to achieve health and wholeness. Together we can find healing for your hurting heart.

In loving-kindness,

Your Great Physician

He will wipe every tear from their eyes.
There will be no more death or mourning
or crying or pain, for the old order of
things has passed away.
Revelation 21:4 NIV

Search me, O God, and know my heart;
test my thoughts.
Psalm 139:23 TLB

Keep your heart with all diligence,
For out of it spring the issues of life.
Proverbs 4:23 NKJV

The LORD is close to the brokenhearted
and saves those who are crushed in spirit.
Psalm 34:18 NIV

The kind of sorrow God wants makes
people change their hearts and lives. This
leads to salvation, and you cannot be
sorry for that. But the kind of sorrow
the world has brings death.
2 Corinthians 7:10 NCV

Our proud confidence is this: the
testimony of our conscience, that in
holiness and godly sincerity, not in fleshly
wisdom but in the grace of God, we have
conducted ourselves in the world,
and especially toward you.
2 Corinthians 1:12 NAS

My Coming Kingdom

*I have prepared a
place for you.*

Dear Blessed Child,

Your human mind cannot imagine the place I have prepared for you and those who have received My love! Look around you at the most beautiful places on earth—majestic, snow-peaked mountains; lush, wildflower-strewn meadows; delightful seascapes; magnificent sunsets—these are nothing compared to Heaven!

For I am the Creator of the universe, and My power and vision far exceed anything you have ever seen. And because I dearly love My children and look forward to spending eternity with them, I have executed My most brilliant and creative works right here in Heaven. It is something to behold! So the next time you feel you're missing out on something special on this earth, be assured, great heavenly wonders await you—so incredible that even the greatest earthly pleasure will never even come close to comparing!

In all creativity,

The Designer of Heaven

Be ready; for the Son of Man is coming at
an hour that you do not expect.
Luke 12:40 NAS

He who hears My word and believes in
Him who sent Me has everlasting life,
and shall not come into judgment, but
has passed from death into life.
John 5:24 NKJV

Your goodness and unfailing kindness
shall be with me all of my life, and
afterwards I will live with you
forever in your home.
Psalm 23:6 TLB

Let them praise the name of the LORD,
For His name alone is exalted;
His glory is above the earth and heaven.
Psalm 148:13 NKJV

Then the kingdom and dominion,
And the greatness of the kingdoms
under the whole heaven,
Shall be given to the people,
the saints of the Most High.
His kingdom is an everlasting kingdom,
And all dominions shall serve
and obey Him.
Daniel 7:27 NKJV

I Can Transform Your Mind

Your mind is becoming more like Mine.

Dear One,

Don't make the mistake many people have made, placing too much importance on "achievements" like fame, power, and wealth. I appreciate qualities like wisdom, humility, servanthood, and generosity. They have substance, and they are incorruptible.

Let Me transform your mind to perceive life from a higher perspective. Quiet your heart and learn to listen to My voice. Meditate on My teaching, and slowly, but certainly, you will receive real and lasting wisdom, insight, and understanding.

With all wisdom,

The Lord Your God

The fear of the LORD is the beginning of
wisdom, and knowledge of
the Holy One is understanding.
Proverbs 9:10 NIV

You will keep him in perfect peace,
Whose mind is stayed on You,
Because he trusts in You.
Isaiah 26:3 NKJV

As we live in God, our love grows more
perfect. So we will not be afraid on the
day of judgment, but we can face him
with confidence because we are like
Christ here in this world.
1 John 4:17 NLT

As he thinks within himself, so he is.
He says to you, "Eat and drink!"
But his heart is not with you.
Proverbs 23:7 NAS

Wisdom, like an inheritance, is a good
thing and benefits those who see the sun.
Wisdom is a shelter as money is a shelter,
but the advantage of knowledge is this:
that wisdom preserves the life
of its possessor.
Ecclesiastes 7:11-12 NIV

Transformation

In your lives you must think and act like Christ Jesus. Christ himself was like God in everything, but he did not think that being equal with God was something to be used for his own benefit. He gave up his place with God and made himself nothing. He was born to be a man and became like a servant. And when he was living as a man, he humbled himself and was fully obedient to God, even when that caused his death—death on a cross. So God raised him to the highest place. God made his name greater than every other name so that every knee will bow to the name of Jesus—everyone in heaven, on earth, and under the earth. And everyone will confess that Jesus Christ is Lord and bring glory to God the Father.

Philippians 2:5-11 NCV

If any of you lacks wisdom, let him ask of God, who gives to all generously and without reproach, and it will be given to him.

James 1:5 NAS

Your attitude should be the kind that was shown us by Jesus Christ.
Philippians 2:5 TLB

My little children, again I feel the pain of childbirth for you until you truly become like Christ. I wish I could be with you now and could change the way I am talking to you, because I do not know what to think about you.
Galatians 4:19-20 NCV

You are living a brand new kind of life that is continually learning more and more of what is right, and trying constantly to be more and more like Christ who created this new life within you.
Colossians 3:10 TLB

WHO HAS KNOWN THE MIND OF THE LORD, THAT HE WILL INSTRUCT HIM? But we have the mind of Christ.
1 Corinthians 2:16 NAS

The beginning of wisdom is this: Get wisdom, and whatever else you get, get insight.
Proverbs 4:7 NRSV

I Know What's Best

Sometimes things happen that you don't understand.

Dear One,

I know that when death, loss, or tragedy strike, you sometimes question whether I really know what I'm doing—if I'm really in control. When you feel that way, come to Me with your questions, lay your doubts and your heartaches at My feet. Together we will examine each one, and I will give you the strength and courage to face every trial and tribulation. I am not the author of your pain, but I am the dresser of your wounds.

And so, dear one, when tragedy strikes, I encourage you to come directly to Me. And don't be afraid to vent your grief and frustration. For, believe Me, I can take it—I have wide shoulders to cry on, and I long to comfort you.

Ready to help,

Your Blessed Redeemer

Praise be to the God and Father of our Lord Jesus Christ, the Father of compassion and the God of all comfort, who comforts us in all our troubles, so that we can comfort those in any trouble with the comfort we ourselves have received from God.

2 Corinthians 1:3-4 NIV

We know that in all things God works for the good of those who love him, who have been called according to his purpose.
Romans 8:28 NIV

We are pressed on every side by troubles, but not crushed and broken. We are perplexed because we don't know why things happen as they do, but we don't give up and quit. We are hunted down, but God never abandons us. We get knocked down, but we get up again and keep going.
2 Corinthians 4:8-9 TLB

The Lamb who is in the midst of the throne will shepherd them and lead them to living fountains of waters. And God will wipe away every tear from their eyes.
Revelation 7:17 NKJV

The LORD is near to the brokenhearted, and saves the crushed in spirit.
Psalm 34:18 NRSV

121

Your Hope Is in My Hand

Sometimes life seems hopeless.

Dear Beloved,

I have an enemy, dear friend. And when you align yourself with Me, this enemy becomes yours as well. My enemy seeks to destroy all hope. And, indeed, as I look about the earth, I see many whose hope is languishing or almost dead. That's why it's so imperative that you put your hope in Me. For only here, in Me, can your hope survive and thrive and grow stronger. It's almost inevitable that all earthly sources of hope will fail you at one time or another—but I will never fail you. Your hope is safe in Me.

Once you've securely placed your hope in Me, I can show you how to be hopeful in many situations. For My hope infiltrates all areas of your life. It will lighten your spirit and encourage your heart. My hope allows you to see difficult situations in a positive light—and this can bring hope to others, too.

With assurance,

The God of Hope

His delight is in the law of the LORD,
And in His law he meditates day and night.
Psalm 1:2 NAS

I will sing of your strength,
in the morning I will sing of your love;
for you are my fortress,
my refuge in times of trouble.
Psalm 59:16 NIV

The LORD is good to those
who wait for Him,
To the soul who seeks Him.
Lamentations 3:25 NKJV

Let us hold fast to the confession of our
hope without wavering, for he who
has promised is faithful.
Hebrews 10:23 NRSV

Hope does not disappoint, because the
love of God has been poured out within
our hearts through the Holy Spirit
who was given to us.
Romans 5:5 NAS

This I call to mind and therefore I have
hope: Because of the LORD's great love we
are not consumed, for his
compassions never fail.
Lamentations 3:21-22 NIV

Hope

We work hard and suffer much in order
that people will believe the truth, for our
hope is in the living God, who is the
Savior of all people, and particularly of
those who believe.
1 Timothy 4:10 NLT

May our Lord Jesus Christ himself and
God our Father, who loved us and through
grace gave us eternal comfort and good
hope, comfort your hearts and strengthen
them in every good
work and word.
2 Thessalonians 2:16-17 NRSV

You have this faith and love because of
your hope, and what you hope for is kept
safe for you in heaven. You learned about
this hope when you heard the message
about the truth, the Good News that
was told to you.
Colossians 1:5-6 NCV

In your hearts set apart Christ as Lord.
Always be prepared to give an answer to
everyone who asks you to give the reason
for the hope that you have. But do this
with gentleness and respect.
1 Peter 3:15 NIV

No one whose hope is in you
will ever be put to shame,
but they will be put to shame
who are treacherous without excuse.
Psalm 25:3 NIV

The Spirit of the Sovereign LORD is on me,
because the LORD has anointed me
to preach good news to the poor.
He has sent me to bind up the
brokenhearted,
to proclaim freedom for the captives
and release from darkness
for the prisoners.
Isaiah 61:1 NIV

Know that wisdom is thus for your soul;
If you find it, then there will be a future,
And your hope will not be cut off.
Proverbs 24:14 NAS

It Will Get Better

*Disappointment
diminishes over time.*

Dear One,

I have watched you suffer disappointments. I've seen you cringe beneath their sharp, cruel blows. And like an earthly father, I long to cradle you in My arms and reassure you that you'll be okay and that before long you will feel better. Being the God of eternity, I understand what a healing balm time can be to these wounds. So, I encourage you, My child, come to Me, and allow Me to heal your hurts.

If you let Me, I can even use your disappointments to strengthen you—to help you grow into the person I created you to be. Because nothing gets wasted with Me. I delight in transforming hardship into glory. And I can do it with you.

With compassion,

Your Heavenly Father

His anger is but for a moment,
His favor is for life;
Weeping may endure for a night,
But joy comes in the morning.
Psalm 30:5 NKJV

We can rejoice, too, when we run into problems and trials for we know that they are good for us—they help us learn to be patient. And patience develops strength of character in us and helps us trust God more each time we use it until finally our hope and faith are strong and steady.

Romans 5:3-4 TLB

Those who sow in tears
will reap with songs of joy.
Psalm 126:5 NIV

No discipline seems pleasant at the time,
but painful. Later on, however, it
produces a harvest of righteousness and
peace for those who have
been trained by it.
Hebrews 12:11 NIV

As a mother comforts her child,
so I will comfort you; you shall be
comforted in Jerusalem.
Isaiah 66:13 NRSV

By Your Love

Dear Precious One,

Who can really understand the true meaning of love? Perhaps it's because so little of it is seen in practice. But that's where you come in, My child. For consider the way I have loved you—unconditionally, totally, eternally. That is just how I want you to love others.

First, I want you to love them whether they deserve it or not, for that's the way I love you. Next, I want you to love them genuinely, for there is no profit in empty words. And finally, I want you to continue to love them with strength and consistency. Okay, I know this all sounds overwhelming, for you are, after all, human. But that's where I come in. If you come to Me and ask for My help, I can love others through you. So, please, come to Me, and let Me teach you to love, one little step at a time.

All My love,

The Lord of All

A new command I give you: Love one another. As I have loved you, so you must love one another.
John 13:34 NIV

Love each other with brotherly affection and take delight in honoring each other.
Romans 12:10 TLB

In everything set them an example by doing what is good. In your teaching show integrity, seriousness and soundness of speech that cannot be condemned, so that those who oppose you may be ashamed because they have nothing bad to say about us.
Titus 2:7-8 NIV

Our proud confidence is this: the testimony of our conscience, that in holiness and godly sincerity, not in fleshly wisdom but in the grace of God, we have conducted ourselves in the world, and especially toward you.
2 Corinthians 1:12 NAS

If you really fulfill the royal law according to the Scripture, "You shall love your neighbor as yourself," you do well.
James 2:8 NKJV

Your Serving Heart

Put others above yourself.

Dear One,

It's only human to think of yourself first, placing your needs above others. But, as you know, My ways are higher than that. If you really wish to be like Me, learn to place others above yourself. For in the same way that My Son came to earth to serve all humanity, so I desire that My children become experts at serving one another.

And for that reason I wish to reveal the secret to a truly fulfilling life. As you may have guessed, it comes from serving others. But here's where the mystery lies. You see, you cannot simply serve for the purpose of serving. No, like most of My promises, there is a heart connection here, too. For it's only when you serve others out of a heart of love, mercy, and compassion that the real miracles take place. And so, once again, I encourage you to come and learn from Me. For I know all there is to know about serving.

Your servant,

The Lord God Almighty

Humble yourselves in the sight of the
Lord, and He will lift you up.
James 4:10 NKJV

Whoever wishes to become great among
you shall be your servant.
Matthew 20:26 NAS

You are not to be like that. Instead, the
greatest among you should be like the
youngest, and the one who rules like the
one who serves.
Luke 22:26 NIV

If anyone serves Me, let him follow Me;
and where I am, there My servant will be
also. If anyone serves Me,
him My Father will honor.
John 12:26 NKJV

Don't be selfish; don't live to make a good
impression on others. Be humble, thinking
of others as better than yourself.
Philippians 2:3 TLB

Serve wholeheartedly, as if you were
serving the Lord, not men.
Ephesians 6:7 NIV

You Cannot Serve Two Masters

Sometimes you get pulled in other directions.

Dear One,

I know you experience many demands and pulls on your life. And often your attention is divided among various things. Most are important—responsibilities like family and career and the basics of daily living. But I want you to understand that nothing is more important than your relationship with Me. Why? Because your relationship with Me strengthens and fortifies you, making you able to deal with all the other aspects of your life.

When you come to Me first and draw from the resources I provide for you, then you can do a better job of managing and caring for all the other elements of your life. So, in love, I encourage you to keep Me first and uppermost in your life, and then everything else will fall neatly into place.

Your Lord and King,

The Almighty

⊗⊗

This is love: that we walk in obedience to
his commands. As you have heard from
the beginning, his command is
that you walk in love.

2 John 6 NIV

*What does the LORD your God require
from you, but to fear the LORD your
God, to walk in all His ways and love
Him, and to serve the LORD your God
with all your heart and with
all your soul.
Deuteronomy 10:12 NAS*

No one can serve two masters. Either he
will hate the one and love the other, or he
will be devoted to the one and despise the
other. You cannot serve both
God and Money.
Matthew 6:24 NIV

If you love me, obey me; and I will ask
the Father and he will give you another
Comforter, and he will never leave you.
John 14:15 TLB

The LORD redeems
the soul of His servants,
And none of those who trust in Him shall
be condemned.
Psalm 34:22 NKJV

Loyalty

Be very careful to observe the
commandment and the law which Moses
the servant of the LORD commanded you,
to love the LORD your God and walk in all
His ways and keep His commandments
and hold fast to Him and serve Him with
all your heart and with all your soul.
Joshua 22:5 NAS

Shout with joy before the Lord, O earth!
Obey him gladly; come before him,
singing with joy.
Try to realize what this means—the Lord
is God! He made us—we are his people,
the sheep of his pasture.
Go through his open gates with great
thanksgiving; enter his courts with praise.
Give thanks to him and bless his name.
Psalm 100:1-4 TLB

Never be lacking in zeal, but keep your
spiritual fervor, serving the LORD.
Romans 12:11 NIV

Whenever we have an opportunity, let us
work for the good of all, and especially for
those of the family of faith.
Galatians 6:10 NRSV

Of this gospel I have become a servant
according to the gift of God's grace that was
given me by the working of his power.
Ephesians 3:7 NRSV

You can see that I am not trying to please you
by sweet talk and flattery; no, I am trying to
please God. If I were still trying to please men
I could not be Christ's servant.
Galatians 1:10 TLB

You shall walk after the LORD your God and
fear Him, and keep His commandments and
obey His voice; you shall serve Him
and hold fast to Him.
Deuteronomy 13:4 NKJV

Whoever speaks, is to do so as one who is
speaking the utterances of God; whoever
serves is to do so as one who is serving by the
strength which God supplies; so that in all
things God may be glorified through Jesus
Christ, to whom belongs the glory and
dominion forever and ever. Amen.
1 Peter 4:11 NAS

Give Your Fear to Me

My love melts away fear.

My Own,

I know you experience fear from time to time. Sometimes it leaps out and catches you unaware, its clutches tight and threatening. Other times, it seeps like a vapor into your heart, growing there like a sickly cancer. Whichever way it comes, it is never from Me, dear child, for I will never rule you with fear. Instead I will guide you lovingly.

For, you see, My love is designed to annihilate your fear. When you rest securely in My love, you can feel Me watching over you—knowing beyond all doubt that you are safe in My hands. That's when fear evaporates. For My love will not allow it to remain. The next time fear slithers into your life, remember how much I love you. Rest in My love, and watch your fear simply fade away.

In perfect love,

Your Heavenly Father

I sought the LORD, and he answered me; he delivered me from all my fears.
Psalm 34:4 NIV

Even if you should suffer for what is
right, you are blessed. "Do not fear what
they fear; do not be frightened."
1 Peter 3:14 NIV

There is no fear in love; but perfect love
casts out fear, because fear involves
punishment, and the one who fears
is not perfected in love.
1 John 4:18 NAS

Their ships are tossed to the heavens and
sink again to the depths; the sailors cringe
in terror. They reel and stagger like
drunkards and are at their wit's end. Then
they cry to the Lord in their trouble, and
he saves them. He calms the storm and
stills the waves. What a blessing is that
stillness, as he brings
them safely into harbor!
Psalm 107:26-30 TLB

The LORD replied, "My Presence will go
with you, and I will give you rest."
Exodus 33:14 NIV

Take Courage, My Child

I will strengthen you.

Dear One,

Sometimes you see a trial or challenge heading your way, and you want to turn and run in the other direction. It's a natural response, My child. But I want you to view these tests and hardships from a different perspective. I want you to understand how the results of these trials can actually be quite rewarding.

Consider how an athlete trains himself by pushing and challenging his body, even to the point of severe pain, but the result is his ability to endure and finally reach his goal. So it is with you. As you go through hard times (with My help, to be sure), you become stronger and more capable. Your confidence grows, and you begin to welcome new challenges—for you know that you (and I) can conquer them.

Victoriously,

Your Trainer and Coach

It was good for me to be afflicted so that I might learn your decrees.
Psalm 119:71 NIV

You, O LORD, will keep them;
You will preserve him from this
generation forever.
Psalm 12:7 NAS

Jesus ignored their comments and said to
Jairus, "Don't be afraid. Just trust me."
Mark 5:36 TLB

You have not received a spirit of slavery
leading to fear again, but you have
received a spirit of adoption as sons by
which we cry out, "Abba! Father!"
Romans 8:15 NAS

My future is in your hands.
Rescue me from those who hunt me
down relentlessly.
Psalm 31:15 NLT

Be of good courage,
And He shall strengthen your heart,
All you who hope in the LORD.
Psalm 31:24 NKJV

My Holy-Spirit Helper

I send My Spirit to comfort and encourage.

Dear Beloved,

I wonder if you know about the priceless gift I have given you—My Holy Spirit to help. My Spirit is known as the Comforter and the Helper because He's such a source of encouragement to your spirit. When you hear Me speaking to you, it's His voice that is bringing you My message. He's like My very own love letter written right on the pages of your heart.

But to reap the full benefits, you must read this love letter, and you must respond to the prompting of My Spirit. For then you will find (as we enjoy this close-knit relationship) that you experience more power, more self-control, and more personal victory than ever before. So allow My Spirit to lead you, and just see where we will go!

With power and might,

The Lord Your God

Don't you know that you yourselves are
God's temple and that God's Spirit
lives in you?
1 Corinthians 3:16 NIV

*When the Helper comes, whom I shall
send to you from the Father, the Spirit of
truth who proceeds from the Father, He
will testify of Me.*
John 15:26 NKJV

Do not quench the Spirit.
1 Thessalonians 5:19 NKJV

My Holy Spirit shall not leave them, and
they shall want the good and hate the
wrong—they and their children and their
children's children forever.
Isaiah 59:21 TLB

Do you not know that your body is a
temple of the Holy Spirit, who is in you,
whom you have received from God?
You are not your own.
1 Corinthians 6:19 NIV

As one whom his mother comforts, so I
will comfort you; and you shall be
comforted in Jerusalem.
Isaiah 66:13 NAS

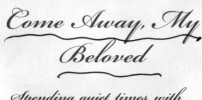

Come Away, My Beloved

*Spending quiet times with
Me will change your heart.*

Dear One,

Oh, how I delight when we spend time alone together, My child. Just you and I, without the distractions of the day pressing in upon us. For it's in those moments that I can whisper My words of grace and love for you. I can share My wisdom and even give personal direction for your daily life. But best of all, I can transform your heart.

For, it is true, only as you come before Me in quietness and truth can I transform your heart. And a heart transformed is an amazing thing— one of life's greatest miracles! When your heart is changed and strengthened and made whole, it affects every area of your life. As My love begins to radiate through you—even your countenance changes! So, come away with Me, My beloved. Spend time alone with Me. And just see what happens!

He who loves you most,

Your Father in Heaven

When you pray, go into your room, close the door and pray to your Father, who is unseen. Then your Father, who sees what is done in secret, will reward you.
Matthew 6:6 NIV

Look! I have been standing at the door and I am constantly knocking. If anyone hears me calling him and opens the door, I will come in and fellowship with him and he with me.
Revelation 3:20 TLB

Now about prayer. When you pray, don't be like the hypocrites who love to pray publicly on street corners and in the synagogues where everyone can see them. I assure you, that is all the reward they will ever get. But when you pray, go away by yourself, shut the door behind you, and pray to your Father secretly. Then your Father, who knows all secrets, will reward you.
Matthew 6:5-6 NLT

Pray to the LORD for the city where you are living, because if good things happen in the city, good things will happen to you also.
Jeremiah 29:7 NCV

Prayer

The Spirit helps us in our weakness; for we
do not know how to pray as we ought, but
that very Spirit intercedes with sighs too
deep for words.
Romans 8:26 NRSV

I say to you, whatever things you ask
when you pray, believe that you receive
them, and you will have them.
Mark 11:24 NKJV

For this reason, all who obey you
should pray to you while they still can.
When troubles rise like a flood,
they will not reach them.
Psalm 32:6 NCV

Pray in the Spirit on all occasions with all
kinds of prayers and requests. With this in
mind, be alert and always keep on praying
for all the saints.
Ephesians 6:18 NIV

Remember, your Father knows exactly
what you need even before you ask him!
Matthew 6:8 TLB

This is the confidence we have in
approaching God: that if we ask anything
according to his will, he hears us. And if
we know that he hears us—whatever we
ask—we know that we have what
we asked of him.
1 John 5:14-15 NIV

The righteous cry out, and the LORD hears,
and delivers them
out of all their troubles.
Psalm 34:17 NKJV

What should I do then? I will pray with
the spirit, but I will pray with the mind
also; I will sing praise with the spirit, but I
will sing praise with the mind also.
1 Corinthians 14:15 NRSV

Then you will call upon Me and come and
pray to Me, and I will listen to you.
Jeremiah 29:12 NAS

I Will Give You Rest

Come to Me when you are weary.

My Dear Child,

I know how My children get weary. Even you can begin to slow down and lose your zest for life. But remember—when your steps start to lag behind and you feel that old heaviness weighing upon your shoulders, it is time to come to Me, and I will give you rest. My rest, unlike earthly rest, can restore you in a moment.

For the instant you bring your troubles to Me, your heart immediately grows lighter, your spirit lifts, and you become energized! Suddenly you are ready to continue, for you are resting in Me—and My rest can sustain you! But I desire that you not only come to Me, but that you also walk with Me, for then I will be able to teach you to pace yourself, to respond to My lead and prevent that kind of weariness that drains your spirit. So come to Me and walk with Me—and I will give you rest.

Your rest,

The Lover of Your Soul

Come to Me, all who are weary and heavy-laden, and I will give you rest. Take My yoke upon you and learn from Me, for I am gentle and humble in heart, and YOU WILL FIND REST FOR YOUR SOULS. For My yoke is easy and My burden is light.

Matthew 11:28-30 NAS

He makes me to lie down
in green pastures;
He leads me beside the still waters.
Psalm 23:2 NKJV

I am like a tree whose roots reach the
water, whose branches are
refreshed with the dew.
Job 29:19 NLT

Your love has given me great joy and
encouragement, because you, brother,
have refreshed the hearts of the saints.
Philemon 7 NIV

My soul finds rest in God alone; my
salvation comes from him. He alone is my
rock and my salvation; he is my fortress,
I will never be shaken.
Psalm 62:1-2 NIV

My people will live in a peaceful
habitation, and in secure dwellings and in
undisturbed resting places.
Isaiah 32:18 NAS

Rest

It is a sign between Me and the sons of
Israel forever; for in six days the LORD
made heaven and earth, but on the seventh
day He ceased from labor, and was
refreshed.
Exodus 31:17 NAS

Thus says the LORD:
"Stand in the ways and see,
And ask for the old paths, where the
good way is,
And walk in it;
Then you will find rest for your souls."
Jeremiah 6:16 NKJV

He who dwells in the secret place of the
Most High shall abide under the
shadow of the Almighty.
Psalm 91:1 NKJV

God who cheers those who are discouraged
refreshed us by the
arrival of Titus.
2 Corinthians 7:6 TLB

So I said, "Oh, that I had
wings like a dove!
I would fly away and be at rest."
Psalm 55:6 NKJV

For this reason we have been comforted.
And besides our comfort, we rejoiced even
much more for the joy of Titus, because
his spirit has been refreshed by you all.
2 Corinthians 7:13 NAS

Let us do our best to go into that place of
rest, too, being careful not to disobey God
as the children of Israel did,
thus failing to get in.
Hebrews 4:11 TLB

God, you sent much rain;
you refreshed your tired land.
Psalm 68:9 NCV

Count Your Blessings

Everything good in your life
comes from My hand.

Dear Beloved One,

I don't want you to forget how I provide for you, My child, or for you to take any of your many blessings for granted. For when you overlook even the small, simple things, you can begin to lose your spirit of gratitude. Now, I don't need your gratitude to feel good (although I do delight in grateful hearts), but I know that being thankful is healthy for your sake!

When you acknowledge the good and wonderful things in your life, you experience a sense of contentment, gratitude, and awe. Your heart is happy! And that makes Me happy, too. So take notice—look all around you—and count your blessings. See how I give good gifts to My children. And rejoice!

With loving benevolence,

Your Heavenly Father

Every good and perfect gift is from above,
coming down from the Father of the
heavenly lights, who does not change
like shifting shadows.
James 1:17 NIV

As for every man to whom God has given riches and wealth, and given him power to eat of it, to receive his heritage and rejoice in his labor—this is the gift of God. For he will not dwell unduly on the days of his life, because God keeps him busy with the joy of his heart.
Ecclesiastes 5:19-20 *NKJV*

We should not be like cringing, fearful slaves, but we should behave like God's very own children, adopted into the bosom of his family, and calling to him, "Father, Father." For his Holy Spirit speaks to us deep in our hearts, and tells us that we really are God's children. And since we are his children, we will share his treasures—for all God gives to his Son Jesus is now ours too. But if we are to share his glory, we must also share his suffering.
Romans 8:15-17 TLB

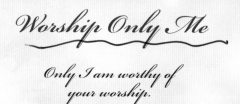

Worship Only Me

Only I am worthy of your worship.

Dear Child of Mine,

If you observe people all over the world, you will find that all desire to worship something or someone. Unfortunately, along their life journey, they may begin to worship things. Some may bow down before fame, fortune, knowledge, experience—things that will never make them truly happy.

And occasionally, you may fall into this trap, too. You may focus your attention and desires upon something other than Me, the Creator of all. Mankind is my highest creation—only man and woman were created in My own image. So how can it be right to worship something less than yourself. I am the only one higher and the only one worthy of your worship.

Your one and only,

The Lord of All

Oh come, let us worship and bow down;
Let us kneel before the LORD our Maker.
Psalm 95:6 NKJV

*I am Jehovah your God who liberated
you from your slavery in Egypt.
You may worship no other god than me.*
Exodus 20:2-3 TLB

Then he said to them, "Watch out! Be on
your guard against all kinds of greed; a
man's life does not consist in the
abundance of his possessions."
Luke 12:15 NIV

I will bless you as long as I live, lifting up
my hands to you in prayer.
Psalm 63:4 TLB

Every created thing which is in heaven
and on the earth and under the earth and
on the sea, and all things in them,
I heard saying,
"To Him who sits on the throne, and to
the Lamb, be blessing and honor and
glory and dominion forever and ever."
Revelation 5:13 NAS

Worship

Praise the LORD.
How good it is to sing praises to our God,
how pleasant and fitting to praise him!
Psalm 147:1 NIV

Great is the LORD, and greatly to
be praised
In the city of our God,
In His holy mountain.
Psalm 48:1 NKJV

Since we are receiving a kingdom that
cannot be shaken, let us be thankful, and
so worship God acceptably with
reverence and awe.
Hebrews 12:28 NIV

God is Spirit, so those who worship him
must worship in spirit and in truth.
John 4:24 NLT

For you who fear my name the sun of
righteousness shall rise, with healing in its
wings. You shall go out leaping
like calves from the stall.
Malachi 4:2 NRSV

Then Moses and the Israelites sang this song to the LORD: "I will sing to the LORD, for he is highly exalted. The horse and its rider he has hurled into the sea. The LORD is my strength and my song; he has become my salvation. He is my God, and I will praise him, my father's God, and I will exalt him."
Exodus 15:1-2 NIV

We who worship God in the Spirit are the only ones who are truly circumcised. We put no confidence in human effort. Instead, we boast about what Christ Jesus has done for us.
Philippians 3:3 NLT

The secret things in their hearts will be made known. So they will bow down and worship God saying, "Truly, God is with you."
1 Corinthians 14:25 NCV

Jesus replied, "We must worship God, and him alone. So it is written in the Scriptures."
Luke 4:8 TLB

Turn Away from Evil

*Learn to recognize and
resist temptation.*

Dear One,

As I have mentioned, trials are a normal part of this life and often serve as opportunities to grow and learn. Temptation, on the other hand, is something quite different. Although everyone experiences temptation at times, it is something I want you to learn to quickly recognize and walk away from—without looking back!

The best way for you to become adept at recognizing temptation is to be filled with My Spirit and to walk daily and consistently with Me. For I send early warnings to My children, and I always provide a way to escape temptation's eager clutches. Stick with Me, and I will be able to help you resist temptation and avoid a great deal of misery and heartache. The reward is great: a heart free, at peace, and abounding in joy!

Delivering you,

Your Deliverer and Redeemer

The good man brings out of his good
treasure what is good; and the evil man
brings out of his evil treasure what is evil.
Matthew 12:35 NAS

I have thought much about your words,
and stored them in my heart so that they
would hold me back from sin.
Psalm 119:11 TLB

He who keeps instruction is in the way of
life, but he who refuses correction
goes astray.
Proverbs 10:17 NKJV

Be self-controlled and alert. Your enemy
the devil prowls around like a roaring lion
looking for someone to devour.
1 Peter 5:8 NIV

Since he himself has gone through
suffering and temptation, he is able to
help us when we are being tempted.
Hebrews 2:18 NLT

He told them, "Pray God that you will not
be overcome by temptation."
Luke 22:40 TLB

Cast Your Cares on Me

Let Me carry your worries for you.

Dear One,

The world around you flows abundantly with trouble and distress, and because this generation thrives on information, I often witness My children bombarded by all kinds of stressful and disheartening news. I know how this negativity can lead to anxiety and inner turmoil. For as you focus on the problems (whether they be personal or global), you subsequently remove your eyes from Me. And you temporarily forget what I am able to do.

So, the next time you feel fretful or anxious, just consider it a signal, a reminder that it's time to run to Me and lay your worries at My feet! Ask Me to help, ask Me to bring about change, ask Me for hope and healing—and for miracles. Come to Me with all your worst dreads and fears and see what I am able to do!

In My hands,

Your Heavenly Father

Look at the birds of the air; they do not sow or reap or store away in barns, and yet your heavenly Father feeds them. Are you not much more valuable than they? Who of you by worrying can add a single hour to his life?

Matthew 6:26-27 NIV

*Be anxious for nothing, but in
everything by prayer and supplication
with thanksgiving let your requests be
made known to God.*
Philippians 4:6 NAS

Do not worry about tomorrow, for
tomorrow will worry about itself. Each
day has enough trouble of its own.
Matthew 6:34 NIV

Don't be troubled. You trust God,
now trust in me.
John 14:1 NLT

The Spirit of the Lord GOD is upon Me,
Because the LORD has anointed Me
To preach good tidings to the poor;
He has sent Me to heal the
brokenhearted,
To proclaim liberty to the captives,
And the opening of the prison to
those who are bound.
Isaiah 61:1 NKJV

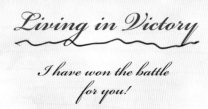

Living in Victory

*I have won the battle
for you!*

Dear Child of Mine,

I know how times can come when you might feel that life is just one great, big battlefield—and sometimes you wonder who's really winning. Without a doubt, there are spiritual forces waging against My children and My creation. My enemy is definitely your enemy—and his goal is to wreak havoc in your life.

But you need to remember that I am the victor! For I defeated My enemy, once and for all, when My Son died on the cross and rose from the grave. And I invite you to celebrate My victory with Me and live in that confidence. Unfortunately, My enemy doesn't acknowledge My victory and remains in the attack mode. For that reason you need to stick close to Me and utilize My protection. But be assured, I have already won the war—and I share My victory with you!

Victoriously,

The King of Kings

Do you not know that in a race all the
runners run, but only one gets the prize?
Run in such a way as to get the prize.
1 Corinthians 9:24 NIV

As you abound in everything—in faith,
in speech, in knowledge, in all diligence,
and in your love for us—see that you
abound in this grace also.
2 Corinthians 8:7 NKJV

In Your mercy cut off my enemies,
And destroy all those who afflict my soul;
For I am Your servant.
Psalm 143:12 NKJV

I strain to reach the end of the race and
receive the prize for which God is calling
us up to heaven because of what
Christ Jesus did for us.
Philippians 3:14 TLB

The LORD loves the just and will not
forsake his faithful ones. They will be
protected forever, but the offspring
of the wicked will be cut off.
Psalm 37:28 NIV

The LORD is my strength and song.
Exodus 15:2 NKJV

Victory

Commit yourself to the LORD; let Him
deliver him;
Let Him rescue him, because He
delights in him.
Psalm 22:8 NAS

Today the LORD your God has commanded
you to obey all these laws and regulations.
You must commit yourself to them
without reservation.
Deuteronomy 26:16 NLT

You became our followers and the Lord's;
for you received our message with joy
from the Holy Spirit in spite of the trials
and sorrows it brought you.
1 Thessalonians 1:6 TLB

Since he himself has gone through
suffering and temptation, he is able to help
us when we are being tempted.
Hebrews 2:18 NLT

Pray God that you will not be
overcome by temptation.
Luke 22:40 TLB

The Lord knows how to rescue the godly
from temptation, and to keep the
unrighteous under punishment for
the day of judgment.
2 Peter 2:9 NAS

The LORD answer you in the
day of trouble!
The name of the God of Jacob
protect you!
May he send you help from the sanctuary,
and give you support from Zion....
May he grant you your heart's desire,
and fulfill all your plans.
May we shout for joy over your victory.
Psalm 20:1-2,4-5 NRSV

I will sing of thy power; yea, I will sing
aloud of thy mercy in the morning: for
thou hast been my defence and refuge in
the day of my trouble.
Psalm 59:16 KJV

My Lasting Treasure

What matters most eternally?

Dear Loved One,

It is nearly impossible for you to understand the true dimensions of eternity. Your human brain isn't designed to comprehend such vast things. But your heart occasionally gets a brief glimmer of what's to come. Tucked deep into your spirit is the understanding of immortality— I planted it there when you were only a spark of life and mere energy.

But now I want you to try to understand what is most important to Me about eternity. I want you to know where My treasure lies. It is you, My child. You are My most valuable treasure. You are what I live (and died) for. Eternal fellowship and relationship with you is worth more to Me than anything in the entire universe. I want to spend eternity with you, in a place that radiates with promise and life and joy!

Forever yours,

The Lord God

The LORD appeared to him from afar,
saying, "I have loved you with an
everlasting love; therefore I have drawn
you with lovingkindness."
Jeremiah 31:3 NAS

Day by day the Lord also pours out his
steadfast love upon me, and through the
night I sing his songs and pray to
God who gives me life.
Psalm 42:8 TLB

God, who is rich in mercy, because of His
great love with which He loved us, even
when we were dead in trespasses, made us
alive together with Christ (by grace
you have been saved).
Ephesians 2:4 NKJV

I love them that love me; and those that
seek me early shall find me.
Proverbs 8:17 KJV

Keep yourselves in the love of God; look
forward to the mercy of our Lord Jesus
Christ that leads to eternal life.
Jude 21 NRSV

Having been justified by His grace we
should become heirs according
to the hope of eternal life.
Titus 3:7 NKJV

I'll Show You My Will

I can direct your life.

Dear One,

Sometimes you question where your life is going, and you wonder if I am even guiding you at all. But it's during those times that you need to ask yourself, are you really following Me? For how can I lead you where you will not follow?

You need to remember that I seldom (hardly ever!) reveal My complete will for anyone's life in specific detail or very far into the future. That's because I know it could possibly overwhelm you, or it might encourage you to employ a wrong strategy for getting there. It might even destroy your incentive and make you think you should just sit back and do nothing. For these reasons (and more) I impart My will to you one piece at a time. Then I expect you to partner with Me to get there. But, oh, what a joyous journey it can be as you travel with Me in trust—discovering My will for you—one day at a time.

Still leading,

He Who Loves You

Your words are a flashlight to light the
path ahead of me, and keep
me from stumbling.
Psalm 119:105 TLB

If they obey and serve Him,
They shall spend their days
in prosperity,
And their years in pleasures.
Job 36:11 NKJV

The things you have learned and received
and heard and seen in me, practice these
things, and the God of peace
will be with you.
Philippians 4:9 NAS

If you obey my commands, you will
remain in my love, just as I have obeyed
my Father's commands
and remain in his love.
John 15:10 NIV

Anyone who does God's will is my
brother, and my sister, and my mother.
Mark 3:35 TLB

The world and its desire are passing away,
but those who do the will of
God live forever.
1 John 2:17 NRSV

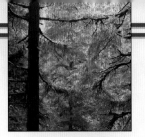

Direction

When the Spirit of truth comes, he will
lead you into all truth. He will not speak
his own words, but he will speak only
what he hears, and he will tell you
what is to come.
John 16:13 NCV

If anyone chooses to do God's will, he
will find out whether my teaching
comes from God or whether I speak
on my own.
John 7:17 NIV

Help me to do your will, for you are my
God. Lead me in good paths, for
your Spirit is good.
Psalm 143:10 TLB

It is God's will that your good lives should
silence those who make foolish
accusations against you.
1 Peter 2:15 NLT

You are free from the law, but that doesn't mean you are free to do wrong. Live as those who are free to do only God's will at all times.
1 Peter 2:16 TLB

He who searches our hearts knows the mind of the Spirit, because the Spirit intercedes for the saints in accordance with God's will.
Romans 8:27 NIV

Patient endurance is what you need now, so you will continue to do God's will. Then you will receive all that he has promised.
Hebrews 10:36 NLT

Lead me in the path of your commands, because that makes me happy.
Psalm 119:35 NCV

For this reason, since the day we heard it, we have not ceased praying for you and asking that you may be filled with the knowledge of God's will in all spiritual wisdom and understanding.
Colossians 1:9 NRSV

You Look Like Me

*Daily, I am making you
in My image.*

My Own,

With a new baby, everyone studies his features, wondering who he most looks like. Great parental pride is extracted from discovering familial similarities. I am no different, My child. I delight as I notice how, more and more, you are beginning to look like Me.

Can you see it, My child? Do you notice how your heart has become more loving; how your speech is more seasoned with grace; how your countenance is softened with gentleness and patience? Perhaps it's something that only a Father can see. But I can certainly see it in you, dear one. And it makes Me beam with fatherly pride. So continue growing in Me. And, in time, others will see the striking resemblance—and one day, you'll see it, too. Because you are My child, and I am in you!

With joy,

Your Heavenly Father

∞

Those God foreknew he also predestined
to be conformed to the likeness of his Son,
that he might be the firstborn among many
brothers. And those he predestined, he also
called; those he called, he also justified;
those he justified, he also glorified.

Romans 8:29-30 NIV

I exhort you, be imitators of me.
1 Corinthians 4:16 NAS

The person who has been born into God's
family does not make a practice of
sinning, because now God's life is in him;
so he can't keep on sinning, for this new
life has been born into him and controls
him—he has been born again.
1 John 3:9 TLB

I will be a Father to you, and you will be
my sons and daughters, says the
Lord Almighty.
2 Corinthians 6:18 NIV

Then Jesus said to His disciples, "If
anyone desires to come after Me, let him
deny himself, and take up his cross,
and follow Me."
Matthew 16:24 NKJV

I'll Never Leave You

*My faithfulness is more
constant than the tide.*

Dear One,

People in this world come and go—some move on as quickly as they came. And it's inevitable that everyone gets left behind now and then. That is simply the transient nature of earthly life. But I am not like that, My child.

For I will never, never leave you. My love for you is constant and unconditional. Even if you ceased to love Me, I would never stop loving you. And I loved you before you even knew Me. A good human metaphor for My love is that of parent and child; yet even that analogy is inadequate, for sometimes a parent is separated from a child. But I will never separate Myself from you. Even if it feels like I am not there, I am. I will never leave you!

Forever yours,

Mighty God

No man shall be able to stand before you
all the days of your life; as I was with
Moses, so I will be with you. I will not
leave you nor forsake you.
Joshua 1:5 NKJV

172

The LORD himself goes before you and will be with you; he will never leave you nor forsake you. Do not be afraid; do not be discouraged.
Deuteronomy 31:8 NIV

I am convinced that neither death, nor life, nor angels, nor principalities, nor things present, nor things to come, nor powers, nor height, nor depth, nor any other created thing, will be able to separate us from the love of God, which is in Christ Jesus our Lord.
Romans 8:38-39 NAS

I will ask the Father, and he will give you another Counselor, who will never leave you.
John 14:16 NLT

The LORD says, "This is my agreement with these people: My Spirit and my words that I give you will never leave you or your children or your grandchildren, now and forever."
Isaiah 59:21 NCV

173

Faithfulness

We will never forsake you again.
Revive us so we can call on your
name once more.
Psalm 80:18 NLT

Let love and faithfulness never leave you;
bind them around your neck,
write them on the tablet of your heart.
Proverbs 3:3 NIV

That which we have seen and heard we
declare to you, that you also may have
fellowship with us; and truly our
fellowship is with the Father and
with His Son Jesus Christ.
1 John 1:3 NKJV

God is faithful; by him you were called
into the fellowship of his Son,
Jesus Christ our Lord.
1 Corinthians 1:9 NRSV

My Presence will go with you,
and I will give you rest.
Exodus 33:14 NIV

If I take the wings of the dawn,
If I dwell in the remotest part of the sea,
Even there Your hand will lead me,
And Your right hand will lay hold of me.
Psalm 139:9-10 NAS

You are My friends if you do whatever I
command you. No longer do I call you
servants, for a servant does not know
what his master is doing; but I have called
you friends, for all things that I heard
from My Father I have made
known to you.
John 15:14-15 NKJV

He is close to all who call
on him sincerely.
Psalm 145:18 TLB

Because of the LORD's great love we are
not consumed, for his compassions never
fail. They are new every morning; great is
your faithfulness.
Lamentations 3:22-23 NIV

Come Stand on Your Rock

I will not be moved.

Dear One,

Everything on earth is constantly changing. Even huge mountains are known to tremble and shake and actually move. But, I am immovable. I am constant and solid—more steadfast than the Rock of Gibraltar. I cannot be pushed aside or shoved off to another position.

And so it is with My attributes and My character. My love is constant. My grace is immovable. My forgiveness is complete. I am the living rock upon whom you can build your life. I am the strong foundation on which you can rely and trust. So anchor yourself to Me, dear one, and you will be able to withstand the darkest, fiercest storms of life. Even if Heaven and earth pass away, and they will one day, I will remain—as strong and constant as ever. If you are anchored to Me, then you will remain as well.

Steadfast,

The Rock of Your Salvation

He reached down from heaven and took me and drew me out of my great trials. He rescued me from deep waters.
Psalm 18:16 TLB

*Everyone who hears these words of mine
and puts them into practice is like a wise
man who built his house on the rock.
The rain came down, the streams rose,
and the winds blew and beat against that
house; yet it did not fall, because it had its
foundation on the rock.*
Matthew 7:24-25 NIV

You are my hiding place; You preserve
me from trouble.
Psalm 32:7 NAS

Who but our God is a solid rock?
Psalm 18:31 NLT

The works of his hands are faithful and
just; all his precepts are trustworthy. They
are steadfast for ever and ever, done in
faithfulness and uprightness.
Psalm 111:7-8 NIV

Know therefore that the LORD your God,
He is God, the faithful God, who keeps
His covenant and His lovingkindness to a
thousandth generation with those who
love Him and keep His commandments.
Deuteronomy 7:9 NAS

Steadfastness

The Lord is my fort where I can enter and
be safe; no one can follow me in and slay
me. He is a rugged mountain where I hide;
he is my Savior, a rock where none can
reach me, and a tower of safety. He is my
shield. He is like the strong horn of a
mighty fighting bull.
Psalm 18:2 TLB

He only is my rock and my salvation,
my stronghold; I shall not be shaken.
on God my salvation and my glory rest;
the rock of my strength,
my refuge is in God.
Psalm 62:6-7 NAS

The firm foundation of God stands, having
this seal, "The Lord knows those who are
His," and, "Everyone who names the
name of the Lord is to abstain
from wickedness."
2 Timothy 2:19 NAS

The Lord is faithful, who will establish
you and guard you from the evil one.
2 Thessalonians 3:3 NKJV

In his kindness God called you to his
eternal glory by means of Jesus Christ.
After you have suffered a little while, he
will restore, support, and strengthen you,
and he will place you
on a firm foundation.
1 Peter 5:10 NLT

Who is God except the LORD? Who but
our God is a solid rock?
2 Samuel 22:32 NLT

In this way they will lay up treasure for
themselves as a firm foundation for the
coming age, so that they may take hold
of the life that is truly life.
1 Timothy 6:19 NIV

The works of his hands are faithful and
just; all his precepts are trustworthy. They
are steadfast for ever and ever, done in
faithfulness and uprightness.
Psalm 111:7-8 NIV

This Will Strengthen You

*Your faith increases
with use.*

Dear Beloved,

Times will come when it seems as if the whole world is falling apart. You will look around and wonder how this planet can possibly survive another single day. And that's when you need to stand firm. That's when I want both of your feet planted securely in the faith I have given you. That's when I want you to remain steadfast and immovable in My love and grace and to continue trusting that I am still in control.

An amazing thing will happen as your faith remains firm—others will take notice. For your steadfast confidence will stand out like a beacon against the dark backdrop of instability and chaos. Like a magnet, you will draw others as they look to you for strength and stability. And that's when you can direct their attention to Me. And together we can rescue them!

Partnering with you,

The Mighty One

Happy is the man who doesn't give in and
do wrong when he is tempted, for
afterwards he will get as his reward the
crown of life that God has promised those
who love him.

James 1:12 TLB

*My dear brothers, stand firm. Let
nothing move you. Always give
yourselves fully to the work of the Lord,
because you know that your labor in
the Lord is not in vain.*
1 Corinthians 15:58 NIV

That does not mean we want to tell you
exactly how to put your faith into
practice. We want to work together with
you so you will be full of joy as you
stand firm in your faith.
2 Corinthians 1:24 NLT

With all these things in mind, dear
brothers, stand firm and keep a strong
grip on the truth that we taught you in
our letters and during the time
we were with you.
2 Thessalonians 2:15 TLB

You too, be patient and stand firm,
because the Lord's coming is near.
James 5:8 NIV

Your Happiness Is in Me

The pleasures of this world will pass away, but I will remain.

My Own,

Many people spend their entire lives in search of true happiness—but what they don't always realize (until the end) is that true happiness is found only in Me. In the meantime, they may be distracted by the dogged pursuit of adventure or fortune or fame; but even if they do find these things (and few do), they will quickly discover that such pleasure is fleeting.

But you are becoming wiser, dear one, for you are beginning to realize that true happiness is a state of heart that comes from being My child. It is not a consequence of a picture-perfect life. It is the direct result of a healthy and continuing relationship with Me. Despite life's circumstances, My happiness comes wrapped up in My love, peace, and joy. So, once more, I invite you to come to Me. Allow Me to fill you with My happiness—again and again! And then let's dwell there together!

Joyfully yours,

The Lord of All

Wisdom is a tree of life to those who eat
her fruit; happy is the man who
keeps on eating it.
Proverbs 3:18 TLB

Happy is the man who doesn't give in
and do wrong when he is tempted, for
afterwards he will get as his reward the
crown of life that God has promised
those who love him.
James 1:12 TLB

Give great joy to those
who have stood with me in my defense.
Let them continually say,
"Great is the LORD,
who enjoys helping his servant."
Psalm 35:27 NLT

My people shall be satisfied with My
goodness, says the LORD.
Jeremiah 31:14 NKJV

All glory to God, who is able to keep you
from stumbling, and who will bring you
into his glorious presence innocent of
sin and with great joy.
Jude 24 NLT

At last I shall be fully satisfied;
I will praise you with great joy.
Psalm 63:5 TLB

Happiness

Happy is the man who finds wisdom,
And the man who gains understanding.
Proverbs 3:13 NKJV

Praise the Lord! For all who fear God and
trust in him are blessed beyond expression.
Yes, happy is the man who delights
in doing his commands.
Psalm 112:1 TLB

I will go to the altar of God,
to God who is my joy and happiness.
I will praise you with a harp,
God, my God.
Psalm 43:4 NCV

His master replied, "Well done, good and
faithful servant! You have been faithful
with a few things; I will put you in charge
of many things. Come and share
your master's happiness!"
Matthew 25:23 NIV

You too should be glad and
rejoice with me.
Philippians 2:18 NIV

This is the day the Lord has made. We
will rejoice and be glad in it.
Psalm 118:24 TLB

Let all those who seek You rejoice
and be glad in You;
Let such as love Your salvation
say continually,
"The LORD be magnified!"
Psalm 40:16 NKJV

Be glad in the LORD and rejoice,
you righteous;
And shout for joy, all you upright in heart!
Psalm 32:11 NKJV

Let all who take refuge in You be glad,
Let them ever sing for joy;
And may You shelter them,
That those who love Your name may
exult in You.
Psalm 5:11 NAS

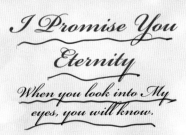

I Promise You Eternity

When you look into My eyes, you will know.

Dear Loved One,

What is the very best gift I can give you? How can I most eloquently express My abounding love for you, dear one? I know I have given you much already—life and love and beauty and joy. But all those gifts are not enough—not nearly. And they are insufficient to convey the greatness, the vastness of My amazing love for you.

That is why I created eternity. It is My finest gift to you ever! It is the prize My Son paid for when He laid down His life, and it is undoubtedly the very best I can offer (and that is no small thing!). Oh, how I delight to give this gift. For I know how earthly life can be difficult at times. I have witnessed My children's struggles through heartbreaks and sorrows and unanswered questions. But eternity with Me is the reward for your pain and suffering! And, I promise you, dear child, it is well worth the effort! So hope in Me, My child, and hope in eternity. For when you look directly into My eyes, it will all fall into place!

Forever yours,

Your Loving Father

I am the Alpha and the Omega, the First and the Last, the Beginning and the End.
Revelation 22:13 NIV

Do not let your heart be troubled; believe in God, believe also in Me. In My Father's house are many dwelling places; if it were not so, I would have told you; for I go to prepare a place for you. If I go and prepare a place for you, I will come again and receive you to Myself, that where I am, there you may be also.

John 14:1-3 NAS

"I am the A and the Z, the Beginning and the Ending of all things," says God, who is the Lord, the All Powerful One who is, and was, and is coming again!
Revelation 1:8 TLB

They shall fear You
As long as the sun and moon endure,
Throughout all generations.
Psalm 72:5 NKJV

This is what God has testified: He has given us eternal life,
and this life is in his Son.
1 John 5:11 NLT

Heaven

Keep yourselves in the love of God; look
forward to the mercy of our Lord Jesus
Christ that leads to eternal life.
Jude 21 NRSV

He died for all so that all who live—
having received eternal life from him—
might live no longer for themselves, to
please themselves, but to spend their lives
pleasing Christ who died and rose
again for them.
2 Corinthians 5:15 TLB

All who believe in God's Son have eternal
life. Those who don't obey the Son will
never experience eternal life, but the wrath
of God remains upon them.
John 3:36 NLT

Now that you have been set free from sin
and have become slaves to God, the
benefit you reap leads to holiness,
and the result is eternal life.
Romans 6:22 NIV

*Surely goodness and mercy shall follow
me all the days of my life;
and I will dwell in the house
of the LORD forever.*
Psalm 23:6 NKJV

All who trust him—God's Son—to save
them have eternal life; those who don't
believe and obey him shall never see
heaven, but the wrath of God
remains upon them.
John 3:36 TLB

Since death came through a man, the
resurrection of the dead comes
also through a man.
1 Corinthians 15:21 NIV

Truly, truly, I say to you, he who hears My
word, and believes Him who sent Me, has
eternal life, and does not come into
judgment, but has passed out of
death into life.
John 5:24 NAS

We know that if our earthly house, this
tent, is destroyed, we have a building from
God, a house not made with hands,
eternal in the heavens.
2 Corinthians 5:1 NKJV

If you have enjoyed this book, we invite
you to visit our website to learn about
other Harvest House books and products:

www.harvesthousepublishers.com

HARVEST HOUSE™PUBLISHERS

EUGENE, OREGON